PRESSURE MYTHS

Understanding the Psychology of Performance

RICH HUDSON

D1438575

First Published in March 2018 by RDH00.

Print Edition

A catalogue record for this book is availability from the British Library:

Print ISBN: 978-1-9996335-0-9

CONTENTS

PREFACE

I began studying psychology at school aged 16 and became a qualified cricket coach in the same year. Over the subsequent years, whilst working full-time in cricket coaching, I gained a Master of Science degree in Sport Psychology and progressed through the coaching qualifications, graduating from the England & Wales Cricket Board's Level 4 'Master Coach' programme in 2015.

However, very little of what I was taught about the mind and performance over this time seemed to have any sustainable impact. There were a litany of tips, techniques and strategies that were passed on to athletes, but most made no sense, did not make a difference or if they did, they only had a temporary, almost placebo, effect.

Seemingly out of nowhere, one summer's day I read a tweet recommending a book about an *inside-out* understanding of the mind. I bought it, I read it, it made some sort of sense to me and then it went back onto the bookshelf. Several months later, needing something to pass the time on a flight to Australia, I picked it back off the bookshelf. This time when I read it, its impact was far more profound. I *knew* this was *it* – how the human experience really works.

Pressure Myths attempts to distil much of what I have been fortunate to learn (and relearn) about performance and well-being over the past few years. This book is relevant for performance in all sports and beyond. I hope as many athletes, coaches and parents as possible can enjoy the benefits of sharing in this understanding.

THE FOUNDATIONS

"Life is like any other contact sport. You may encounter hardships of one sort or another. Wise people find happiness not in the absence of such hardships, but in their ability to understand them when they occur."
—Sydney Banks (Philosopher)

INTRODUCTION

There is no one way to think, but there is only one way that the mind works. When we do not understand how our experience is being created through our minds, it can lead to us harbouring a host of assumptions that prevent us from playing our best and enjoying the game for what it is. Therefore, despite athletes being fitter, stronger and faster than ever before, misunderstood thoughts and beliefs continue to get in the way of them performing to their potential.

For example, it seems logical to assume that playing in a World Cup Final is the biggest moment in every player's life, so they need to feel confident but there is a lot of pressure to perform. In reality, a World Cup Final is as big a moment as each individual thinks and believes it is. For one it may be the most important day ever, for another it may be just another day. Whilst confidence is great, every player has performed when they were low on confidence and everyone has failed when they were feeling sky high. Furthermore, although there may be a lot riding on the game externally – the trophy, money, playing in front of a huge crowd and TV audience – the amount of pressure a player feels before or during the game is only a result of their thinking which will fluctuate through the day.

Whether the match is on the village green or in the Test Match arena, understanding how the mind works in a common-sense way can bring about sustainably higher levels of performance and a greater sense of enjoyment. The *inside-out* understanding of the mind explained in this book examines the psychology that drives the characteristics, perspectives and behaviours of peak performance. It explains how we can all get the most out of what we do. It looks at where pressure really comes from – and where it does not – so that we can leave behind the misunderstandings that get in our way. It shows how resilience, confidence and the capacity to perform to our potential reside within each one of us.

There are two illusionary causes (they look and feel real but are not the real cause) of pressure:

- The Game (the challenge or the importance)
- The Consequences (which can lead to a fear of failure or putting pressure on ourselves)

When we believe and are caught up in an illusory cause of pressure, we forget the only true cause of pressure:

- Thought in the moment

This leads to losing sight of our innate performance resources, which are always available if we understand that we have them:

- Confidence
- Resilience
- Motivation
- The capacity to perform however we are feeling

This book shines a light on the illusory tricks of the mind that are so easy to fall into and it points us back to utilising and enhancing the abilities we have. It provides a clearer understanding of these illusions and the innate resources that enable sustainable high performance and grow our love of the game.

We only lose sight of these innate resources when they are covered over by temporary illusory thinking or misunderstood beliefs about pressure. When we understand how the mind works from the inside-out, every individual can identify implications for their own game so that they can perform more effectively and effortlessly when it comes to the crunch.

UNDERSTANDING

When it feels as if the fun has gone out of playing the game or we cannot seem to play our best when we need to, the solution to these problems is a deeper understanding of how those experiences are created in the mind. If we want a different experience of the game, we must first have a different understanding of the game.

EVERYONE'S ACTIONS ARE BASED ON THEIR UNDERSTANDING OF HOW THINGS WORK

Understanding is the key to all of psychology and performance – what we understand determines our thoughts, feelings, perceptions and behaviours. If we understand that fire burns, we will not put our hand into one. If we are on a train and we understand that another train is travelling the other way, on the next set of tracks, we will not put our heads out the window. If we understand that a putting green slopes from left to right, we will play with the lie of the land rather than hitting straight across it.

When we understand that playing sport is more fun (and we feel better) when we have less on our minds, we do less and less thinking that is unhelpful. When we understand that we are always capable of performing, no matter how much we think we are not, then we spend less time worrying about how we are feeling and more time engaged in doing what we do best.

Because understanding is the key to all psychology and performance, it is misunderstanding that limits our experience and potential. When we do not realise that fire will burn us, a train is travelling towards us or how the putting green lies, we will make mistakes based on our misunderstandings. Our decisions reflect our level of understanding.

Having a clear understanding of where our experience comes from is apparent in people who are 'comfortable in their own skin', able to ride the ups and downs of life with grace, have fun, learn, love and do the best that they can, whilst retaining a sense of perspective and humility, however things work out.

Some people 'get it' without being able to put words to it. This is because they never lost this intuitive understanding of how to get the most from life from when they were children.

Small children have yet to pick up the misunderstandings that get in the way of having fun and doing their best, but as time passes, we all collect ideas from our parents, friends, families and society about how the world works, how our minds work and what it takes to be successful. This becomes our conditioning – our worldview.

If we believe that things work a certain way, our world is shaped to reflect this. What we see becomes what we are looking for. How the outside world looks to everyone is based entirely on their thinking about it. If we look for love and learning in any situation, we will find it. If we look for anger and blame, we can always find that too.

Our perceptions and behaviour are a direct result of how we are seeing (or understanding) our world in that moment. If we believe something that is not actually true, we will be trapped by that misunderstanding. This is then reflected in how we perceive the world to be and how we interact within it.

UNDERSTANDING OCCURS NATURALLY

Understanding how the mind works, and experiencing the benefits of that, does not require any fixing, coping mechanisms or techniques. There are no 'to-dos' or 'seven steps to success' programmes required. Psychological skills do not work like physical skills which can be built through practice. They are innate capacities that we realise through an intuitive understanding of them.

Permanent changes to what we think and feel, and how we behave, occur effortlessly through a shift in the level of our understanding. This is not an intellectual process of trying to think our way towards change. It naturally falls into place as we see more clearly where our moment-to-moment experience is really coming from. We gain a deeper understanding every time we have an 'insight' – a thought that creates a natural, effortless shift in how we see the world which brings us closer to reality and further away from misunderstanding. It is a moment when we go from not knowing something to knowing it.

When we see the truth of something insightfully for ourselves, we can see the same thing with a fresh appreciation. Before then it is just another set of ideas, but afterwards it appears as such common-sense that we wonder how we missed it previously.

Insights appear when we have less on our minds. This happens instinctively the more we understand how the mind works. When we have an insight, we have a clearer perspective without trying (e.g. great ideas occurring to us when we are out for a walk or having a shower). As misunderstanding naturally falls away, some of the things we used to think and some of the ways we used to behave stop making sense. This is how people change in a way that is so organic that they only realise it looking back.

The more we understand how the mind works from the *inside-out*, the less we get in our own way. We were born with natural motivation, confidence and resilience. When we appreciate that this is true, we experience them as we did as children, without the limiting habits of thinking that we have collected along the way.

Understanding how the mind works, and the nature of the game that we are playing, enables us to find our own answers that are natural, original and intuitive. When we look beyond our beliefs, biases, difficulties and challenges, we see solutions that, with hindsight, look obvious and feel authentic. This is in stark comparison to the struggle that can ensue when we copy somebody else and hope to achieve the same result.

There is no limit to which we can understand something. Once we think we have it figured out, we may see it again in another way and understand it even more clearly. The deeper our understanding of the mind, and the sports we play, the more straightforward they become to navigate. This natural process of understanding turns what can seem very complicated into effortless simplicity.

> *"A moment's insight is sometimes worth a lifetime of experience."*
>
> *—Oliver Wendall Holmes (Supreme Court Judge).*

OUR PSYCHOLOGICAL SYSTEM

Although we all have different lives, personalities, abilities and beliefs, we all have a psychological system that works the same way for everyone to create their experience.

THE WORLD APPEARS TO DETERMINE HOW WE FEEL

It seems that external factors – e.g. circumstances, situations, people, money, results – make us happy or sad, relaxed or stressed, calm or anxious. This is an 'outside-in illusion'. It appears logical and feels very real, but when we actually consider it, it is not how it works at all.

If our reality was created from the outside-in, then two people in the same situation would always feel exactly the same, but they never do. Similarly, individuals would always feel the same when faced with identical situations multiple times, e.g. always or never nervous when walking onto the field for a game. However, in truth, sometimes we do and sometimes we do not.

When someone cuts us up on the road when driving, it can look like they are causing us to feel angry through their poor driving. Yet not everybody gets angry at other people's bad driving and, if we think about it, we do not feel equally angry every time somebody drives dangerously. Similarly, a horror movie does not cause everyone to feel scared. Even more interestingly, two people can both be feeling scared watching the same film, but one may be hating it and hiding behind their hands while the other is loving it and finding feeling scared to be a real 'buzz'.

WE DO NOT EXPERIENCE THE WORLD DIRECTLY, WE EXPERIENCE OUR THINKING ABOUT THE WORLD

Thought – comprising all conscious and unconscious thinking – is the energy that enables us to experience everything in life. Thought creates our moods, feelings, emotions and perceptions. How we relate to the thoughts that pass through our minds shapes our beliefs, sense of perspective and our overall experience of life from the 'inside-out'.

A situation is unable to generate a feeling and then implant it into our heads, although it undoubtedly often seems this way. As much as the feeling looks like it is coming from the situation, it is not. People experience a range of different emotions because they are experiencing their thinking about the situation, not the situation itself.

Our feelings are coming from thought, and how we relate to those feelings determines whether we find them (e.g. being scared watching the horror movie) thrilling or painful. Everyone falls for the outside-in illusion at times – it is part of being human. Thought creates our perceptions and feelings and, when we fail to recognise where they are coming from, we look outside for a set of circumstances to which we can attribute them.

Problems arise when we believe that a temporary experience of an 'outside-in illusion' is how things actually work and we become victims to our circumstances. This is because we end up attaching our well-being and enjoyment to the achievement of various standards of success. If our lives are going well, we feel good (most of the time) and if our lives are not going so well, we feel bad. Without realising it, we are making up the definition of what a 'good life' is. It is in our nature to be free to feel good and enjoy ourselves however and whatever we are doing.

There is a 100% connection between thought and feeling and a 0% connection between circumstance and feeling. Therefore, feelings of pressure, stress, anxiety, confidence, freedom and concentration can only ever come from the one source – thought.

If we feel under pressure and do not understand the source of the feeling, we are likely to assume it is because of the difficulty, importance or the conse-quences of the game – but it is not. When we feel in 'the zone' we might assume that it is because we put our lucky socks on, did a specific pre-game routine or tried extraordinarily hard – but it is not. When we feel demotivated we look for reasons why the game is not as much fun anymore, but none of them are absolute truths.

Our psychological system only works one way – inside-out – whether we recognise it or not. As we understand the inside-out nature of our experience, some of our existing thinking habits stop making sense. As we react less to our own thinking, we become psychologically freer from the world around us and playing to our potential becomes more straight-forward. By having a deeper understanding of how thought creates our experience, we become more adept at handling the ups and downs of the game and of life in general.

A THOUGHT IS A THOUGHT

All the thoughts we have look and feel real, but they are not. They are transient illusions – energy passing through our minds – providing us with temporary experiences, ideas and perspectives. We can be standing at the top of a cliff and have the thought 'JUMP!' and ignore it. We might even laugh at how crazy the thought was. However, people who see the thought as real will actually jump. We do not have to believe the thoughts that appear to us. A thought is what it is – a thought.

No thought has any inherent meaning or power to make us act a certain way. We can have a thought and not act on it. We can observe it, ignore it or let it go. Alternatively, we can provide it with energy and attention until it becomes a metaphorical fire burning within our minds. Whilst we cannot prevent a negative thought coming into our heads, we do not have to take our thoughts, or anyone else's, too seriously.

We do not get to choose the next thought, feeling or mood that comes into our head – but we can understand it. Thought comes from beyond us. It appears in our consciousness and is then processed by the brain. It is part of the formless energy and intelligence that powers all of life. The intelligence that turns plants towards the Sun, rotates the planets on their axis and brings clouds over a blue sky. This natural intelligence behind life creates and dissolves all things, from the natural world around us to our own thinking.

Our thoughts and moods are always changing – nobody can remember what they were thinking at the same time yesterday. Believing we can control our thinking is a misunderstanding that creates an exhausting process of doing more and more thinking in an attempt to gain control. However, when we let go of trying to control our experience, we automatically find more enjoyment and higher levels of performance without the tiring search.

If we could control our thinking, we would feel on top of the world all the time, but that does not happen because this is not how it works. Nobody would choose to have dark, low and angry thinking plaguing their experience. However, low thoughts provide the yin and yang of life.

We appreciate sunny days when we contrast them with cold, rainy ones (or vice-versa depending on our thinking!). We appreciate feeling free only having experienced feeling pressure, we appreciate feeling love only having experienced pain, we appreciate feeling relaxed only having experienced stress. As we give up the desire to control what we cannot, our outlook shifts and performance flows without us trying.

Everybody's understanding, and experience, of life fluctuates throughout the course of each day (and from day to day). This is because we all experience the natural ups and downs of moods. Moods change naturally of their own accord, providing us with different perspectives of life. As thought builds up and quietens down, our moment-to-moment experience of life shifts, which means the same situation can look another way depending on the mood that we are in. Everybody has different ups and downs of thought and because of that everyone is having a different experience of life.

As our minds become full of thinking, we feel anxious, stressed or insecure. When thought flows naturally, our minds become clearer and we feel better (confident, calm or relaxed). In a low mood everything looks very serious, hard work and pretty bleak. In a high mood, we see the positives, the opportunities and the potential to have fun. The less we have on our minds, the better we feel, but even the happiest person on the planet experiences low moments that thought brings. Low moods are as inevitable and integral to the human psychological system as the rain is to nature's weather system.

THE MIND IS DESIGNED TO SELF-CORRECT TO CLARITY

When our mood drops and we feel low, if we do nothing (i.e. do not add further thinking on top), our mood will rise again. The mind is designed to clear without any effort or trying from us at all, just as the body is designed to heal cuts without us having to think about it. The never-ending rising and falling of our moods is a fundamental part of the human experience. Thought is always changing. We can be overthinking the situation one minute, then engaged and in flow the next, without doing anything at all.

Low moods are only sustained by holding onto thinking and analysing our problems. In a low state of mind, we can try to think as positively as we can about a situation, but it is not going to make much difference. When our mind self-corrects, our perspective changes and we effortlessly experience more positive and optimistic thoughts. This is why the idea to 'sleep on it' when we are agitated is often good advice. We intuitively know that when we are in a different state of mind, that occurs naturally, we will see a situation in another light.

When we understand that we feel better when we have less on our minds, it stops making sense to try to do more thinking to feel better. We allow the mind to clear thought just as we allow the heart to beat blood around our bodies. However, if we have a misunderstanding that we need something to happen for us to feel relaxed or happy, we usually end up trying to think, fix or cope our way out of a low feeling. This only prolongs or worsens the experience. The weight of thinking that causes us to feel low falls off our minds naturally when we stop getting in its way.

Our feelings tell us about the quality of thinking that we have in the moment. Thought and feeling are two sides of the same coin. There is an infallible feedback loop between our emotions and the thinking we are experiencing. If we are feeling low, frustrated, stressed, angry, nervous, anxious or under pressure, that is direct feedback that we not seeing things clearly. It does not mean that what has happened is right (or wrong), but that our perspective is only a reflection of the thinking we have at that time.

No feeling needs to be fixed or changed, because they are our in-built guide to know how clearly we are seeing the world in that moment. When we are feeling negative emotions, they are a signal to stop believing the thoughts that are occurring. We feel low because thought is clouding our minds. There is a lesson in the feeling. As we recognise how thought creates our perceptions of situation, we avoid becoming lost in it. We retain our bearings and a sense of clarity so that common-sense solutions appear to us, enabling us to handle demanding situations.

WHO WE ARE IS MORE PROFOUND THAN OUR EGO, OUR IDENTITY AND OUR PERSONALITY

When we take away everything that we think – our ideas, beliefs, concepts about ourselves, about others and about life in general – and everything that we have – our accomplishments, relationships, talents, possessions – then what is left is who we really are.

We all have a body, thoughts occurring inside of our minds, successes and failures, and a story about what we think everything means. However, none of those things are who we are. What we are at the most fundamental level is the awareness that can see all of those things and then realise that we are more than all of that, and therefore, not reliant upon it.

Everybody has an 'ego' – a set of ideas about who we are and what we have to do to prove ourselves. This shows up in our personality which is made up of patterns of thinking and behaviour that we have acquired to make sense of the world and navigate within it. This sense of who we are emerges in our thinking as our intellect develops as we grow older. We use our ability to compare, analyse, identify and judge to develop a sense of identity out of the roles we play in life and the thoughts we have about how well we are doing, what else we need, our preferences and what we want other people to think of us.

The ego is who we think we are, rather than who we actually are. Everybody is attached to their ego, personality and identity to a differing degree. Some people believe that these components make up the totality of who they are. Others do not, but we all take these beliefs seriously at times and not at others. Everybody has different personalities, perspectives and abilities, but beyond the level of what we think and how we behave, we are all exactly the same. We are all made up of energy and all experience our lives through the power of thought and consciousness.

Our 'true self' – who we are without all the beliefs and possessions we have collected – is in-built with well-being, confidence and resilience. Losing sight of our deeper nature leads to feelings of insecurity as we identify with our ego, personality and the roles we play. The search to satisfy the feelings of insecurity that occur when we identify ourselves with the thoughts we have, leads to a never-ending pursuit of acquiring external rewards that we hope will make us fulfilled.

As we see who we are on a deeper level, misunder-standings about who we are fall away. We see that who we are is more than the thoughts that pass through our minds and therefore there is always more to life than we think. There is an intuitive intelligence, energy, connection and freedom in all of us at the deepest level.

We will always have ideas about what we must do and what success is. Understanding the ego for what it is loosens our attachment to it. We can then see how our enjoyment and well-being is not contingent on our performances or anything else. We can regain our innate sense of fun and humility, and the capacity for performing and learning that we had when we were younger, without all the layers of misunderstandings about who we think we are.

THE OUTSIDE-IN ILLUSIONS OF PRESSURE

"Thought creates the world and then says 'I didn't do it'."
—David Bohm (Quantum Physicist)

THE GAME

Pressure is a real feeling, but we are only inhibited by it when we misunderstand it. It can look as though the feeling is coming from the game (how difficult or important it is) or other external events, from the consequences (what will happen to us if we succeed or fail) or from other people (their expectations and opinions of us).

From these misunderstandings unhelpful habits of thinking develop, including putting pressure on ourselves and the fear of failure. Believing in any of these illusionary causes of pressure gets in the way of the capacity we already have to play to our potential and enjoy it.

INCREASING THE CHALLENGE OF THE GAME IS AN ESSENTIAL ELEMENT OF SPORT

Difficult and important games or situations often appear to be full of pressure. However, despite their challenges and what can be riding on them, they cannot, on their own, create a feeling of pressure within us. They are illusions that look like they can affect how we feel, but they cannot unless we have a thought that suggests they can and we believe it. There is no pressure inherent in any situation, only within our thinking.

Each game presents a range of challenges for athletes to face. The game-situation, the time left to play, and the precision required to kick, hit or bowl a ball in a given scenario, can all make achieving success harder. Athletes talk about 'trying to build pressure on the opposition', which is an attempt to increase the difficulty of the situation, e.g. a fielding team in cricket restricting the batting team's run-scoring with tight bowling and fielding or a football team relentlessly creating chances which prevents their opposition from regaining their defensive shape.

The harder the game becomes, the less chance the opposition have to win. However, none of these situations can directly lead to us experiencing a feeling of pressure, despite how it can look that way.

'Game pressure', i.e. the difficulty, challenge or timing within the match, will always fluctuate independent of the 'psychological pressure' we experience. Some players experience increased feelings of pressure as their chances of winning increase. They feel more on edge because their thinking begins to race with ideas of what winning would mean, or how they cannot afford to lose from the position they are in. For other players, the feeling of pressure decreases as their chances improve. When they get close to the finish line they are so engaged in what they are doing that all other thinking falls away.

There is an assumption that as the difficulty increases so will the feelings of pressure, which in turn will lead to opponents making a mistake. In reality, whilst we can increase the difficulty of the task, we cannot put a person under the feeling of pressure. If the game situation becomes increasingly more challenging, the opponent is only going to be negatively affected by it psychologically if they have a thought that makes them feel panicked, they believe it and then act on it.

Just because we have a thought does not mean that we have to act on it. If a batsman has the thought "I must hit the next ball for 6" or a footballer has the thought "I must shoot from anywhere" they are not compelled to act on it any more than any other thought. Believing and acting on panicked thinking is unlikely to help in tricky situations. If we intuitively understand (i.e. without trying to consciously comprehend or decipher it) that the game situation is not creating the feeling of pressure, then as we see the thought or feeling for what it is, we will retain our bearings. When we realise that we do not have to act on panicked thinking, we will instinctively find effective solutions, even when the game becomes more challenging.

To develop the skills required to succeed, our abilities need to be challenged in demanding situations. This allows us to see our abilities as they are and to learn and grow from the experience. To do this, preparation and training sessions may have specifically manipulated conditions that suit some players more than others, just as competitive matches do (e.g. playing on surfaces prepared to be more suited to passing teams in football or for serve and volley players in tennis).

These scenarios allow training to be as realistic to the game as possible so that we can develop the skills to adapt to, and win games in, a variety of situations and conditions. Practicing difficult aspects of the game will improve our skills, but it has nothing to do with experiencing or dealing with pressure because situations do not have the power to create emotions.

It is easy to assume that as we go up the 'levels' it will feel more difficult, but that is not always the case. There are plenty of players who get better the higher they go because their abilities become more suited to the 'elite' level than playing lower down the pyramid. The complete opposite can also happen. Different levels require different skills and players can have different thinking that gets in the way of them performing. A player moving up might have the thought 'I'm not ready', whilst somebody dropping down might think 'I'm too good for this'. Having these thoughts is not a problem unless we believe they are truths, rather than understanding that they are idle thoughts.

The challenge of a situation only feels overwhelming when we get so caught up in the feeling of pressure that we forget how resilient we really are. In a low state of mind caused by a congestion of thought, the challenge always appears to be more difficult and appears to make us feel under pressure. It starts to feel as if we *need* to perform. In a different state of mind, the challenge may look tough but manageable, and in another, the situation may seem like an opportunity, fun or that we have nothing to lose.

What feels like pressure depends only on the thinking we have in the moment. There are infinite alternative perspectives that we can see the situation from. It is not that we need to see the situation in any particular way, but to understand that all of the possible ways of seeing it only result from thought in the moment, which is continually changing. We do not need to be gripped by any illusion that thought creates. As thought changes, so will our perspective.

WE ARE NEVER FAZED BY THE 'BIG' OCCASION – ONLY BY OUR OWN THOUGHTS ABOUT IT

The World Cup Final can feel as though it is not only the most important match, but also the most important thing in the entire world. This is because we (athletes, coaches, the media, fans and administrators) collectively construct its importance and buy into the illusion. It is easy to assume, that because so many people believe that the World Cup is extremely important, there will be more pressure. However, the World Cup Final is only as important as we think it is. We create its level of importance in our own minds.

Believing that one thing is more important than another is an unconscious process of taking one thought and placing it above another in a hierarchy. At the higher levels of sport, there will be more people interested, more media coverage, more money available to earn, bigger crowds and stronger opposition. Despite this, some players naturally and intuitively treat all the matches they play in exactly the same, from the Premier League and Test Matches to warm-up matches and friendlies. Others play some games as if they do not matter at all and then seek to raise their game for what they perceive to be the big occasion. Without realising, we decide that 'this' matters and that 'this' does not. Neither is right or wrong, but often we miss the role of thought in determining what matters and what does not.

Playing in a Test Match, at the Olympics, in the Premier League or any other elite level cannot automatically create any more feelings of pressure than playing in the backyard. There are athletes who feel under a lot of pressure when there seems to be more at stake and there are athletes who feel none in this situation. It has nothing to do with the difficulty, importance, crowd, media, money or the level. It just really, really looks that way.

How important a game feels comes from within. This is why playing at a recreational standard can feel extremely important to someone at that level, while international athletes can be totally relaxed about a 'big game'. It is wrapped up in our beliefs and expectations about how good we are, what success is and how important it is to succeed. These are all subjective, an interpretation based on the thinking we have had.

Whether playing at the elite level is more important than playing in the backyard depends on how we look at it. We may think sport is the most important thing in the world. However, we all know someone who thinks sport is just people running around kicking a ball about. Who is right? Neither of us. Our thinking equals our perspective. Their thinking equals their perspective. The power is in realising that thought is the source of our perspective, because then we can never be a victim of it.

Knowing how important a game feels is only ever coming from within us, allows us to create meaning when it feels rewarding to be temporarily emotionally invested in an outcome, e.g. believing that winning the World Cup Final is the most important thing in the world. However, if our perception of how important the game feels leads to us getting consumed in agitated thinking, we are also free to let go of the idea and simply play the game as it comes.

If we believe certain games can create feelings of pressure then we will do more thinking about those games in an attempt to handle, fix or avoid either the situation or the thinking itself. Just because there are more supporters, more media interest and more money at stake does not mean that we have to build the game up to be something more than it is. All these external factors can make it seem that the situation we find ourselves in is very important, but the game is still the same.

When we strip away all the hype and the ideas we have about what winning or losing means, we can play the game as a game. This is true whether it is the World Cup Final or kickaround in the park. We might find ourselves pleasantly surprised by how we adapt and adjust through our sporting endeavours when we see that how we feel about the game, and its challenges, is not coming from the game at all, but only from our thinking about it.

ATHLETES WHO APPEAR TO BE 'LIVING THE DREAM' CAN FEEL AN ENORMOUS AMOUNT OF STRESS

When we get lost in our thinking about the important or difficult it is to perform, we feel stressed. How well we do on the field can feel extremely important because there are results, status, prize money and selection at stake. If we unknowingly assume that whether we attain those rewards or not affects our self-worth, the more thinking we will do about them. However, our feelings and emotions do not actually know how well we are playing or how important our situation is, they are only a reflection of the thinking we are taking seriously in that moment.

The circumstances of our lives (e.g. being a sportsperson) do not insulate us from being human. Feeling stressed is the result of being overwhelmed with the amount of thinking on our minds. Everybody feels stressed when their thoughts are spinning at a million miles an hour. Feeling stressed is not inherently a problem (some people love it). It is the resistance to those feelings that turns it into an issue, as we do more and more thinking about the situation we are in and about how we want to change the feeling of stress.

Stress is a natural part of the spectrum of feelings that make up the human experience. It becomes a habit when we believe that the game is the cause of our feelings of well-being. When we do not appreciate that thought is the only source of an initially transient feeling of stress, it can appear logical to think more about it, analysing what to do and how to do it or try to avoid certain situations. However, this only creates further feelings of stress as thinking piles up.

When we have a thought about the game in a low state of mind, and believe it, then have another thought and another and believe those too, we end up carrying around all those layers of thinking with us, without realising they began only as temporary, illusionary thoughts. We can become so accustomed to a habitual feeling of stress that we only notice it when we finally drop all the thinking we have been carrying around – e.g. going on holiday to relax but ending up spending the whole time ill, as the body finally gets time to recover from all the tension caused by stressful thinking.

Everyone is prone to over-thinking occasionally. The more we believe that there are external reasons for how we feel, the more we will overthink as we habitually analyse and try to fix whatever it is that looks like it is causing us to feel how we are. Stress and worry are simply indicators to let go of whatever we are thinking about. If we understand that we have a deeper, intuitive intelligence beyond our capacity for analysis, unnecessary thinking begins to drop automatically. Fresh insights and solutions are more likely to occur as we go about living our lives, rather than when we are deep in rumination and worry.

PUTTING PRESSURE ON OURSELVES

Putting pressure on ourselves is all the thinking we have about how well we think have to play, based on the false idea that we need to perform (and win) to be fulfilled, relaxed or to enjoy ourselves.

WE EXPERIENCE PRESSURE WHEN WE BELIEVE THAT OUR RESULTS DETERMINE HOW WE FEEL AND WHO WE ARE

We collect beliefs about what success is and what it means that can get in the way of playing our best with a sense of freedom. We believe that we need to win in order to be happy. Or that if we succeed, we become a better, more important person. However, if we fail, we will feel low and if we keep losing, it is not only that game that has gone but also our well-being. We do more and more thinking about how well we have to do to feel good and 'beat ourselves up' when we do not match up to those expectations.

The truth is that who we are has *nothing* to do with how well we do. Who we are is more fundamental than any result or performance can possibly be. It is natural to have preferences for what happens and the results we achieve, but it is not helpful to confuse them with who we are and to build a false sense of self around them.

We are not less of person if we lose every game. We are not more of a person if we win every game. This is the case no matter how much other people seem to believe it or behave differently towards us depending on our results – they are simply caught in the illusion that something outside of us determines our value. It is very much possible to *think* that a result impacts on who we are and our self-esteem, but it is only possible on the superficial level of the ego.

Consequences have no ability to affect how we feel other than to the degree that we believe that they do. We can be very fearful of losing before we realise that losing is OK. We will be worried about looking stupid before we see that we do not have to take ourselves too seriously. It can seem very important to succeed right here and now, but later we might realise that we needed to learn the lessons from failing even more.

Most of the things we spend our time worrying about never actually happen. There are also consequences that we fear and yet when we get there, it turns out that we think that those consequences were actually the best thing to happen to us. That is the illusion of thought. Worried thoughts cannot predict the future any better than any other thoughts, but they do distract us from the innate resources we have to respond to what is happening right now.

To understand who we really are is to see beyond all our thoughts about ourselves and what we believe success and failure to be. When we see who we really are, we realise that this exists on a deeper level than the circumstances of our lives and our achievements, bank balances and relationships. Humility, gratitude and enjoyment then emerge effortlessly from this realisation. When we understand this, it does not make as much sense to build up the game and its outcomes to something more than they are, but instead play them for our own enjoyment.

PUTTING PRESSURE ON OURSELVES IS THINKING ABOUT WHAT WE MUST ACHIEVE AND BELIEVING IT TO BE TRUE

The desire to be selected, and to perform as well as we can, are natural. Problems arise when we develop a sense of needing them to fulfil an idea of ourselves that we feel we have to live up to, without seeing that we were the ones who made up how things have to work out in the first place! This misunderstanding becomes inhibiting as we tense up and lose sight of our intuition.

If we assume that we cannot make mistakes, because otherwise we will not perform to the level we expect, or we will not get selected, then we will 'play it safe', believing that it is better to be cautious than to fully express ourselves and risk making a mistake. We become critical of ourselves, analysing every mistake that prevents us from being perfect. Given a choice of opponents we will prefer the easy option, because our inner projection of perfection cannot be 'shown up'. We do so even though it will limit our long-term learning as our game will only grow by facing the toughest players we can and working out what is required to compete with and beat the best.

We 'try too hard' and fail to produce our best perfor-mances because we become fixated on how things *have* to be. Even when we have been successful, we struggle to enjoy it. This is because we are too busy picking out faults or our minds have wandered off to think about what might come next. We over-value the immediate result and dwell on what we perceive to be our faults. We often miss the bigger picture and that playing sport is only one part of our lives.

There is a crucial distinction between the inner drive to be the best we can be and trying to be perfect in order to live up to the ideas we have about ourselves and what we think success is. Putting pressure on ourselves to be perfect or to achieve our perfect goal only serves to act as a limitation on our potential. The pursuit of our potential does not have to come at the expense of having fun and forgiving ourselves for making errors. We can play the game as it comes, without expectations or standards that feel like they *must* be met. When we do, success can happen naturally and instinctively without having to struggle.

IF WE BELIEVE THAT ACHIEVING GOALS CREATES INTERNAL FULFILMENT, WE WILL SET GOAL AFTER GOAL AFTER GOAL IN A QUEST TO EXPERIENCE THE NEXT FEELING OF HAPPINESS

If we pursue goals to find well-being, life becomes a game of 'I will be happy when...' that never ends. Satisfaction becomes only a fleeting experience when one goal is ticked off before the next one begins.

Society and our friends, family, coaches and team-mates might tell us that the definition of success is 'x or y or z', but that is nothing more than one person's idea being taken on by another to the point that we assume that it must be right. We collect all sorts of beliefs as we go through life, most of which we take on without realising, and then live our lives believing they are correct.

Other people's definitions of success are no more valid than any other belief. They are thoughts, without any inherent meaning or truth. If we believe that somebody is better or worse than us, or more or less deserving than us, then that is a belief not a truth. We might find a million reasons that explain why we believe it, but it is still not a truth. It is simply one way of looking at it which we have bought into.

There is no true definition of success. There are no 'steps to success' that we can copy and implement that will automatically lead to the accomplishment. There is no one path that will work for everyone, even if we are all heading to the same destination. We can learn from others, but our path will always be our own. After all, a goal is no more or less than any other thought. A process is no more or less than a sequence of thoughts that we think, or hope, will work.

All athletes work towards goals, but not everybody achieves them. The difference is not who sets better goals or obsesses more about them, but about who gets the most from their ability based on their understanding of performance.

We can take the fun out of what we are doing when we fail to see there is more to performance than achieving one goal after another. If we get stuck in the process of setting and achieving goals, we can lose sight of the fact that our well-being has nothing to do with whether we achieve them or not. If we are completely consumed by achieving goals to improve our life, there is every chance that we will forget to enjoy it. Achievements are only worthwhile, and goals are only useful, when we know that we can be happy whether we achieve them or not.

We can work towards any goal of our choosing, but also be open to where else it might lead. As we begin to see success and goals for what they are – thoughts about the future that we attach meaning to – then they appear with a greater sense of curiosity and adventure, rather than doubt and insecurity. There are times when more analysis creates a clearer picture or direction. However, there are other times when we might just surprise ourselves if we go with the flow, adjust as we go and see how things play out. The purpose of setting goals can move away from feeling like a *need* towards doing whatever feels right.

Goals can be challenging, rewarding or something that just makes sense. Our purpose and enjoyment can evolve naturally rather than feeling that we need to perform to a certain level to be happy. Well-being is understanding that we are OK with or without all of the possessions we have, what we do and how well we perform. It is being OK with both our ups and downs. People with peace of mind are those who know they can be happy for *no* reason and feel low for *no* reason, because that is part of the nature of being human.

THE QUICKEST WAY TO FALL OUT OF LOVE WITH THE GAME IS TO THINK ABOUT, JUDGE AND ANALYSE IT A LOT

When it stops feeling like a game and starts feeling like work, that is the result of over-thinking. We do not have to take the feelings of difficulty, boredom or hard graft seriously. They are temporary low feelings, in which even what we love doing loses its appeal. In this state of mind, it is easy to start attributing reasons why we have lost the love of the game. However, when our mood rises, our connection to the game rises again and what felt like hard work fades away or can be dealt with a greater sense of perspective.

When success feels like a necessity we become lost in a world of anxious 'What ifs?'. "What if I do not have time to warm up?", "What if the conditions aren't in my favour?", "What if I lose?", "What if I make a mistake and everyone thinks I'm rubbish?". It is a very easy habit to fall into when we want to do our best, but one which creates unnecessary anxiety out of sport that we started playing for fun. When negative scenarios start spinning around our minds, we are experiencing a distorted perception of reality. It is a sign to let go, not only of the thinking in the moment, but also the illusory belief that we need to be successful to be fulfilled.

Burnout occurs when we become so convinced that we need to achieve an outcome that we lose sight of everything else. As we strive to become better, we can develop judgmental and overly analytical thinking habits. Relentlessly seeking improvement, without being able to enjoy things for what they already are, will lead to any human being feeling burnt out. We start following the story in our minds about what we have to do or why we have to do it and forget why we started playing in the first place. We then ruminate on our mistakes and push ourselves harder and harder to perform at the level that we have decided we must reach.

This leads to a deterioration in mental and physical health that has a knock-on effect on our relationships, work-life balance, enjoyment and results. We rush around to match up to our made-up expectations, judgements, needs and desires. When our thinking speeds up, it provides a compelling illusion of what it looks like we need to achieve in the game. Instead of following the idea that we need to possess or achieve something outside ourselves to feel good, we can look within to the innate nature of well-being that we already, and always will, have.

By attaching our well-being to the games that we have won or lost, we can never be truly satisfied as one temporary goal is replaced with another. We are too busy evaluating how we are doing and what we need to do next to enjoy ourselves. These patterns of thinking mean we rarely feel satisfied with, or grateful for, what we do have. Believing that our well-being is contingent on our success makes our well-being *feel* contingent on our success, but it is a trick of the mind.

Athletes do not fall out of love with the game because of contract disputes, being dropped or critical media coverage. It is due to the thinking that we engage in. If we think about any of those things enough, the game will quickly start feeling as though it is not worth playing. We fall out of love with the game when we are not matching up to our expectations, without realising we are creating those expectations and judging ourselves based on them. Becoming bored of a sport that we loved is an illusion created by a busy mind. A busy mind overfilling with thoughts of how things should be or about what is happening next.

We can fall into the trap of associating the lows in our state of mind with what is happening in our lives. If we do not realise where our well-being comes from, then it might seem logical to rely on sport to provide us with the (temporary) feelings that already lie at the core of who we are (permanently). Fortunately, our well-being is not dependent on any circumstance because it is innate. The only thing that obscures it is thought, during low moods or through amassing misunderstandings about the nature of well-being.

There will always be days when it does not feel fun. Even if we love the game, it is not going to feel fun and easy in every moment. When our thinking revs up, it feels like a struggle. When our thinking quietens down, it feels like we are playing for fun. That is the ebb and flow of thought – the game has not changed at all.

When we stop searching for well-being outside ourselves, in our results and performances, then thinking about what we *need* to achieve falls away. We can spend more time playing without pre-conceived expectations when we see how they can get in the way of our enjoyment. Our capacity for playing with a sense of fun and freedom however the game plays out then reopens.

THE FEAR OF FAILURE

Wanting to do the best we can, and therefore by definition avoiding failure, is perfectly normal. For example, a batsman not wanting to get out demonstrates a commitment to the team, respect of the game and an enjoyment of batting. However, when that turns into a fear or anxiety that gets in the way of playing our best in competitive situations, we need to fully understand the source of the fear of failure.

THE FEAR OF FAILURE IS ANXIETY ABOUT JUDGEMENT

Everybody wants to do the best they can. However, we begin to fear getting it wrong when we believe that our self-worth is dependent on other people thinking well of us. Most people are not worried about making mistakes *per se*. When we are on our own, we intuitively understand that failure is an integral part of our learning process and that it can be quite fun.

At the skate park, boarders and bikers will spend an entire day making mistakes, immersed and energised by the process. However, as soon as other people are involved – teammates, parents, coaches, fans, the media – we can become anxious about what they think of us and how they will react if we fail or lose.

When we have this anxiety about judgement, instead of failure being something we can learn from, it becomes something to avoid in case somebody judges or criticises us. We play in a safety first and limited manner, seeking to minimise all possibility of making a mistake. Instead of this approach improving our results or enjoyment of the game, we feel increasingly restricted. Believing the thinking that makes us fear failure takes us away from our innate capacity to perform and therefore, makes us more likely to fail.

When we try to protect the self-image that exists in our thinking, we will constantly be on edge about whether other people will perceive us as a failure. If we strongly identify with the ideas about how good we believe we *must* be, then when we are in a low state of mind, we take seriously insecure, judgmental thoughts about "Why aren't I good enough?" or "What if I look stupid?".

When we are feeling low we can become defensive and feel the need to make a lot of excuses to explain why we have not performed well. In this state of mind, we do not want to hear what other people have to say, even if they have the best of intentions, because we are afraid that they will say something that will damage our self-esteem and diminish our self-worth. We try to protect the way that we see ourselves and the way that we want others to see us. These fears stem from assuming that what others think of us determines who we are and our level of well-being.

In that moment, we have identified with our ego and forgotten who we really are. When we realise that our ego is nothing more than a creation of our thinking and not a real entity, then we can drop our attachment to it at any moment and open up to feedback that can help us learn, improve and have more fun. In a certain moment, we may feel that we have failed, but it is impossible for us to ever *be* a failure. Neither an outcome nor an opinion have the power to define us.

OTHER PEOPLE HAVE EXPECTATIONS OF, AND OPINIONS ABOUT, US BUT THEY CANNOT MAKE US FEEL UNDER PRESSURE

Coaches can expect us to train more often, supporters can expect us to perform to a higher level and teammates can expect us to play in a way that suits them. All of these are normal. They might not be ideal, but they should not come as a surprise. Everybody who cares about, or is interested in, our performance has an opinion of us and an expectation of how they think we should play.

Others' expectations or an increased workload cannot make us feel under pressure. Only having a thought that makes those expectations feel inhibiting (e.g. "I must do well because the team is relying on me tomorrow"), and believing it, can do that. If we see the thought for what it is, when we wake up tomorrow we might see the increased expectations and workload as an opportunity or a show of faith from other people.

Opinions, particularly in sport, are a simple interpretation of a complex situation. Our intellect prefers matters in 'black and white' and that is never more prevalent than when it comes to sport. It prefers the simple categorisation of "they're world-class" or "they're completely over-rated" to the nuanced truth.

When we see a player as 'world-class' it is easy to ignore all the times when the athlete has not performed to that level and only focus on when they have. When we see a player as 'over-rated' we will do the complete opposite. This is confirmation bias – we search for evidence that proves that what we already think is correct, ignoring all the counter-evidence. If we had a different understanding of the situation, we would have a different opinion.

Whether we are perceived as 'world-class', 'over-rated' or somewhere in between, there is nothing we can do about it, except recognise that all opinions and expectations that we and others have are only thoughts. No matter how right or wrong they seem, we do not need to take them personally.

Dealing with critical or judgmental comments from other people is not about having to be strong or weak, it is about being open enough to allow them to pass through our minds. We do not have to hold onto, or analyse, somebody else's perspective once they have said it. What other people think of us is an opinion which is a thought that provides one perspective at one point in time. Their opinion is just another thought in the ether amongst the tens of thousands that we process each day.

If someone's viewpoint is helpful and we can learn from them, it is brilliant. However, if it is not, we can let it go. When we are not thinking about it, it is of no relevance to us. If we keep grabbing the thought back and providing it with power and importance, then we end up dwelling on it. Everyone has the intelligence to filter what other people say – whether to listen and learn or to smile and let it go.

WE ALL SEE THE WORLD DIFFERENTLY BECAUSE WE ALL HAVE OUR OWN COLLECTION OF BELIEFS AND EXPECTATIONS THAT WE USE TO INTERPRET EVERYTHING THAT TAKES PLACE IN OUR LIVES

We all filter the world through our thinking, creating a separate reality of the same event. People have expectations and demands of us and we have them of other people, but they are all made-up out of the thinking we have at that time. This does not mean they are true and it almost certainly does not mean they are fair. However, what other people think of us cannot create our state of mind; it is only the thinking that we take seriously about it that does.

Our worldview in each moment reflects our state of mind. We all have our low points and moments where we lose our bearings. If we feel small and do not understand the source of that feeling, we may look to cut others down to the same size. However, when we feel comfortable in our own skin, we see the positives in other people. Negative, unhelpful or hurtful comments are always more of a reflection of the state of mind of the person speaking them, rather than anything we have actually done or need to do.

When we hold onto a grudge, perhaps because someone has said something we have perceived to be hurtful, it is actually us who experiences that resentment and not the person we are thinking about. We have the painful experience of resentment whenever we bring the thought back into our awareness. We become free when we forgive others, because the burden of holding onto the resentful thinking is released.

We can never truly manage the expectations and opinions of others. Trying to do so is akin to trying to put out a never-ending sequence of fires – once we have set one person straight, we need to move onto the next and the next and so on. No matter how much we try, not everybody is going to like or rate us. We can waste a lot of mental energy trying to please everybody. We can be interested in what others think, whilst being able to see that their opinion is made of the same illusory energy that ours is. Fortunately, our self-esteem is not dependent on anyone else's opinion or anything else outside of us. Well-being is always intact when we see through the layers of insecure thinking that we have believed to be true.

People are always going to have their expectations of us and have their own ways of behaving. Because teams are always looking for a competitive edge, these expectations are likely to only increase as we get better and move up the levels. The degree to which this affects us is the amount that we believe it has the power to. It does not mean that other people's expectations are right or that we should never attempt to change the situation. What it means is that when we understand the nature of others' expectations, we are always capable of rising to them, dealing with them or letting them go, depending on what makes the most sense.

TO DEAL WITH OUR FEAR OF FAILURE, WE CREATE A 'COMFORT ZONE'

We all have a comfort zone – it is a collection of thinking that enables familiar tasks to feel manageable or even easy. Within our comfort zone we experience a feeling of safety. However, as we become increasingly content in our comfort zone, we are likely to stop doing what challenges and scares us. It limits the decisions we make and the opportunities we embrace. We become so busy trying to stay in a comfortable feeling by protecting our self-image, that we are afraid to engage with the necessary learning process of trial and error that will make us a better player in the long run, even if it makes us feel uneasy now.

Having thoughts that make us feel anxious, and unknowingly gravitating to thoughts that create a more relaxed feeling, are a natural part of being human. However, we are capable of both enjoying the comfort zone and seeing through this illusion to get to where we want to go. The feeling of insecurity or anxiety about failure is informing us that we are not seeing it clearly. All thinking passes and when it does, we will have a different perspective. We can see the illusory story that is being told within our own minds for what it is and move past it.

It is possible to progress within our comfort zone by chipping away at the task, rather than listening to the thoughts about why something cannot be done. However, ultimately, we will need to take some leaps into the unknown to find how good we are capable of being. The bigger our dreams and aspirations, the more likely it is we will have to keep stepping outside our comfort zone to the point where it becomes second nature.

Moving beyond our comfort zone sometimes requires courage, where, instead of being put off by a thought that makes us feel afraid or anxious, we 'feel the fear and do it anyway'. The more we see that we are capable even when we are feeling anxious or fearful, the more courageous we become. Not because we are feeling courageous or trying to be courageous, but because we know we can act courageously even when we do not feel it.

At other times, we go into challenging, difficult or dangerous situations instinctively without thinking about it. This instinctive action becomes inevitable from a feeling of love, purpose or enjoyment. This happens more often as we see that our capacity to be courageous and brave is limitless. The fear of failure stops making as much sense when we see that the comfort zone and the fear of failure are both made up in our own thinking. As we see that more and more, what we fear or are anxious about shifts of its own accord and our opportunity to excel, with a greater sense of ease, rises.

Nobody ever completely loses a fear of failure or having a comfort zone; but we can understand them more clearly so that the illusions stop getting in the way of playing our best. By stepping into the void outside of what feels comfortable, we realise how many of our limits are self-imposed by having believed a negative or discomforting thought. This is how we can have so many 'that wasn't as bad as I thought it was going to be' experiences.

When we see that our anxious thoughts are not real – no matter how real they feel – we can ignore the cosiness of the comfort zone and the fears we have about leaving it. Seeing past the illusory nature of these anxious thoughts allows us to find where the boundary between impossible and improbable lies. We can embrace new experiences, opportunities, risks and have fun.

"You miss 100% of the shots you don't take."

—Wayne Gretsky (Ice Hockey – NHL all-time record goal scorer).

THE FUTURE IS UNKNOWN AND THAT IS PERFECT

The ego wants everything under control, because the thought of the unknown makes it feel insecure. The ego knows only what it already knows and only wants to know what it can conceive. It is obsessed with predicting the future as a means of trying to quell the insecure feelings. A 'control freak' is somebody who has become so attached to their thoughts about themselves that they need the world to work according to the way that they think it should work. Therefore, they find it distressing to go with the flow.

Attempting to control the future is an impossible task and yet we spend an inordinate amount of time contemplating it. Our attempts to control every little thing only creates even more thinking. This thinking makes us feel more insecure, less connected and more afraid. If we do not realise that this cycle began with our attempt to control rather than the situation we are in, the cycle will continue. We can spend so much time anticipating the future or trying to get others to do what we think will make us feel OK, that we forget to do what matters right now and enjoy what we already have.

We think progress is going to be a relatively straight line from the start to an end point. However, life has a way of creating a path of ups and downs, and successes and lessons, regardless of what we think of them. The future is always unknown. The unknown is inevitable in the most literal sense, as 96% of the universe is made up of a dark energy that scientists are unable to identify. Although trying to control every step of the journey within the limitations of our minds looks compelling, the fact is that we are surrounded by the unknown.

The image of ourselves that we are trying to keep up comes from and fluctuates within our own thinking. As do our perceptions of other people. If we understand this, we stop trying to avoid making mistakes and doing what we think others want, and instead get on with what makes sense for us. When we take our thoughts about who we have to be and how well we have to perform less seriously, we stop worrying about what others will think. It becomes easier to learn from our experiences rather than playing it safe by trying to please other people. This means we can spend more time having fun doing what we want and being more productive without apprehension.

We will never completely know where we are heading in our sporting endeavours or in our lives. Ultimately, how things play out is not entirely down to us. The game tends to flow of its own accord, whether we like it or not. Much like a surfer on a wave, whilst there are more skilled ways of surfing, we do not control the natural forces of the wave. The more a surfer embraces that truth, the more adept they become at riding it.

THE INSIDE-OUT UNDERSTANDING OF PRESSURE

"Pressure doesn't exist. It's an artificial thing that's a cloud that some people carry and some shove away. I choose to shove it away, as it doesn't exist. I enjoy racing because I want to do it. No one's forcing me. What's the worst that could happen? I lose a race?"

—Adam Peaty
(Swimming – Olympic Gold Medallist)

UNDERSTANDING PRESSURE

An understanding of the nature of thought is the hidden dimension of sporting performance. Sport is simple and fun, but if we do not understand how the mind works to create our experience from the inside-out, it can quickly seem complicated and a chore. Understanding how our experience is created is neither a cure to all ills nor cast-iron guarantee of success, but as we see it more clearly, we are grounded back towards reality, allowing us to play with a greater sense of freedom, perspective and motivation.

PRESSURE IS NOT AN ISSUE WHEN OUTSIDE-IN ILLUSIONS STOP MAKING SENSE

Pressure is a transient emotion that we all experience from time to time, a product of our heads getting congested with thought. Pressure, like every other feeling and emotion, is a natural energy that passes through our minds. We feel excessive pressure when we are caught in the illusions that the game or its consequences can control how we feel. The solution is to understand more deeply the nature of what is happening and where the feeling is (and is not) coming from, so that we realise how capable of handling it we really are.

We do not engage with things we know not to be true. When we clearly see the layers of misunderstood thinking that act as a psychological barrier to our best performances, they automatically fall away enabling us to play naturally, instinctively and to enjoy it. Seeing the illusions of pressure for what they are means that we can go into situations that can look to be high pressure – playing in front of big crowds in cup finals with media attention and contracts on the line – and play the game as it comes rather than being deceived into believing these illusions are the cause of our state of mind.

Understanding how the mind works from the inside-out does not mean we will not feel pressure, or be upset, frustrated or disappointed. This is because we all experience fluctuations of thought and all forget, at times, where our emotions are coming from. However, understanding this equips us to navigate effectively from where we are to a solution or simply having peace of mind with the situation.

When we understand that our experience is created from the inside-out, we see that we cannot be a victim, psychologically, of either our circumstances or the way other people think. If we feel like a victim, it is because we have thinking that makes us feel like a victim. We have a story in our minds of how things should be and when reality does not match it, it is easy to look outside for something to blame it on (e.g. the media or the selectors). There are plenty of occasions where we would hope to be in a different situation, but this feeling of being victim is coming only from the story taking place within our thinking. We can always drop that thinking and address our circumstances with a fresh perspective.

PRESSURE IS NOT AN ISSUE WHEN WE REALISE THE INNATE RESOURCES THAT WE ALREADY HAVE

Planet Earth's natural resources include light, air, water, plants, animals, soil, stone, minerals and fossil fuels. A human being's innate resources include confidence, motivation, resilience and the capacity to perform however we are feeling. These innate resources are in-built in everybody, whether we realise it or not, even if thought temporarily obscures them from our sight with the outside-in illusion of pressure.

Unless we believe otherwise and limit ourselves, we are always capable of performing or doing what we want to do, whether or not we are feeling pressure. Like all transient experiences passing through the mind, the feeling of pressure will pass naturally as the mind clears unless we hold it in place with more and more thinking.

When we get on with playing the game without adding more thinking and attempting to cope with or fix the feeling, it comes and then it goes because the mind is designed to self-correct to clarity. Because infinite ways of looking at the game always exist, as we get less caught in seeing one perspective as *real* then the illusion of pressure lessens its hold and our ability to see the situation with more clarity, and to perform, rises.

We do not need to teach small children to be instinctive (they do what they are going to do without thinking about it) or resilient (even when they get very upset, five minutes later they are fine again) or to be motivated (they are naturally interested, curious and do their best). It is innate. We are all this way until our natural resources are so covered with conditioned and misunderstood thinking that we forget the power we have at our disposal.

We lose touch with confidence, resilience and happiness when we do not understand that they are a part of who we are and begin to search for things outside ourselves – performances, money, relationships or achievements – to try to find them again. Regardless of our state of mind, we already have all the psychological capacities we need to handle everything the game throws at us.

CONFIDENCE

In a confident state of mind, we feel great, play the game instinctively and use our common-sense. Confidence is a natural state of being that was part of our experience long before we learned to take ourselves seriously or took on the idea that we need something outside (e.g. money, approval, results) to make us feel OK on the inside.

WE FEEL MORE CONFIDENT WHEN WE HAVE LESS ON OUR MINDS

Feeling confident has nothing to do with thinking positive thoughts. When we have less on our minds, we automatically feel better. Confidence naturally emanates from a relaxed state of mind, where we barely notice the thoughts passing through. Everybody knows how to relax; effortlessly allowing our thinking to fall out of or pass through our minds, just as we do every time we go to sleep. Confidence is what we feel when we are not consciously thinking about what, or how well, we are doing.

Confidence is a natural capacity that we are born with. Small children have very limited abilities and achievements in the world but are still the most confident people on the planet! They are not wracked with doubt and insecurity, because they have not learnt to interfere with the natural processes of the mind. They do not analyse what they are doing. They live life in the moment, have fun and give it their best shot whatever happens.

It is easy to confuse confidence with a certain set of behaviours or trying to put on a 'confident act'. If we try to force these behaviours through willpower, not only are we creating unnecessary hard work for ourselves, but it also feels inauthentic. This is an exhausting process which unfortunately only leads to people seeming smarmy or arrogant. Peace of mind comes from knowing that who we are is always enough, and that we are always OK, whatever the ups and downs we are experiencing.

Being good at sport (or anything else) does not create confidence despite how persuasive that illusion can look. There is no cause and effect relationship between confidence and competence. This is why the best players in the world can be low on confidence, while park players can have total or even delusional belief in themselves.

It means that making a century in cricket, scoring a 30-yard free kick in football or hitting a tennis back-hand pass down the line, cannot make us fulfilled. It can appear that way because in the moment, all our thinking falls away and in being completely connected to what we are doing, feelings of euphoria, joy and peace emerge. That is where the feeling of true, unconditional confidence comes from; the natural state of having a clear mind.

The more we see that confidence is a part of who we are, the more of it we experience. Rather than searching for confidence in our achievements or through external rewards or by trying to think in a certain way, when we realise that it is innate, then we do less and less thinking that gets in its way.

CONFIDENCE DOES NOT COME FROM OUR RESULTS

We are taught that we can get more confidence from things outside ourselves. This can appear to be from being better, from what other people say or from achievements. If we believe that to be true, we innocently learn to make confidence and feeling good contingent on meeting certain conditions. However, if confidence had anything to do with factors outside ourselves, the biggest sports stars would *always* be confident and more confident than everyone else. However, that simply is not the case.

Confidence does not directly cause success, nor can success create confidence. Results, on their own, cannot make us either confident or happy, or low on confidence or unhappy. We can lose a game when high on confidence and we can win one when we have very little. We can lose a game on the back of a run of wins and we can win a game on the back of a sequence of defeats.

What happens for most of us is that when we win, we drop the thinking that says we *needed* to win and therefore we are able to enjoy the moment. It is that clear mind and relaxed feeling that makes us feel happy, as opposed to the analysis and rumination that we often fall into when we lose. It is possible to win or to have had a career best performance and yet feel miserable if we are thinking about something else. On the other side of the coin, a run of defeats cannot, on their own, cause us to feel unhappy.

Slumps in form do not even exist until we think we are in them. Some players think they are in a slump after two bad shots, for others it never occurs to them. Of course, the same is true with 'good form'. Some players let go of all their thinking and relax after a couple of great shots, others feel on edge until they have put together week upon week of good performances.

We can enjoy playing the game whatever the end result. Winning and feeling good may be preferable, but we are OK without them. We do not *need* to win to feel fulfilled and engaged in what we are doing. Our enjoyment of the game is not reliant on our results unless we think it is. Experiencing this new found sense of freedom from our results can actually increase our likelihood of winning, because we simply play the game as it comes, adapting to what is required in each moment.

EVERYBODY LOSES CONFIDENCE, AT TIMES, BECAUSE THOUGHT FLUCTUATES FOR EVERYONE

"Go find yourself a decent player. I am not the guy you're looking for."

—Graeme McDowell (U.S. Open golf champion) speaking to his caddie, Ken Comboy.

It does not matter how good we are or what we have achieved, when our heads are jammed full of noise we will feel low. This is natural. Low confidence is a transient and temporary state of mind unless we fight it or hold it in place. We extend this low feeling when we analyse the reasons that we believe are causing us to feel low and search for solutions to feel better.

As we search for a better feeling, we rev up yet more thinking rather than allowing the mind to self-correct. It is easy to believe our negative thoughts when we are in a low state of mind because they can appear logical, but the doubts are no more real than any other thoughts. If we have had a run of low results or have been dropped from the team and are feeling low on confidence, it is not the situation that is causing us to feel low but all the thinking and analysis we are doing about it.

Confidence fluctuates, regardless of the circumstances of our life. As our mood rises, we feel more confident, more capable and less concerned about possible negative consequences. As our mood falls, we feel more insecure and question ourselves, doubting that we are good enough. This is why we can be the same player, in the same situation, with the same recent form and yet one day be high in confidence and feel low the next. All moods are simply reflections of the flow of thought – none of them are more indicative of our ability or predictive of the future than another.

Like all thoughts, the doubts will flow in and out of our minds if we do nothing with them. If we look at them very closely and find all the reasons why they might be true or why we do not want to be feeling this way, all the additional thinking only adds another layer of misunderstanding to a thought that was passing through. As the layers build up, our innate well-being gets covered by doubts and insecurities that we have believed to be true.

When we do not understand the nature of thought, it can appear logical to attempt to control how we feel and increase our levels of confidence with techniques and more thinking. However, this at best has a placebo effect (i.e. because we think it has had an effect, we feel an effect, but we are misattributing the real source of the change). Then the search for confidence goes on, as the questioning of why we are not feeling confident becomes psychologically paralysing. Thought comes and goes naturally when we are not attaching to expectations of results and beliefs about what makes us feel good.

AS THE WEIGHT OF MISUNDERSTANDING FALLS AWAY, POSITIVITY AND OPTIMISM NATURALLY EMERGE

As we feel more comfortable in ourselves, enthusiasm and positive body language that reflect that feeling inevitably follow. However, when we are busy analysing, judging and criticising, it is inevitable that we will feel low. Confidence drops when our mind is cluttered with thinking. When we understand that thought is holding a low state of mind in place, we drop it as instinctively as we do heavy bags of shopping we have managed to carry from the car to the kitchen.

Negativity falls away by realising that it is not inherently real. It is what we experience when we are in a low mood and we take our perceptions of a situation seriously. It is an interpretation of a situation that we may see completely differently at another time, in another state of mind. We do not have to believe a thought that tells us that we are rubbish or not good enough or that it is not going to work out.

Complaining is a coping strategy that people use to deal with a low mood, when they do not realise that the thoughts that we have in low moods are illusory and that they will pass on their own. If we feel low and attribute the feeling to external reasons why we might feel that way (e.g. the team's problems), complaining feels cathartic as we believe that we are dealing with it. In reality, we are giving attention to a temporarily skewed perspective. If instead of trying to cope with that low feeling, the thoughts flow through our minds then we will see that as our mood rises, we will see the situation another way. Whilst an issue may still exist, it becomes straight-forward to be solution focused and positive with a clearer mind, instead of absorbed in the negativity and believing it to be real.

Positive thoughts are more enjoyable than negative thoughts, but they are no more real. If we believe all our positive thoughts, we become delusional. If we believe all of our negative thoughts we become depressed. Trying to do 'positive thinking' is unhelpful and unnecessary. We can think as many positive thoughts as we like in a low state of mind, but it will make little difference because we are already sub-merged in thought.

When the mind clears as it is designed to, we effort-lessly feel positive. Everyone has their doubts and insecurities, but it is good to know that our level of insecurity derives solely and directly from the doubt-ful and insecure thoughts we have in that moment. We are all going to have negative thoughts, but we do not have to believe them, take them seriously, fix, change, control, watch or accept them. In the end, they are all just thoughts – transient energy passing through our awareness, providing us with the experi-ence of each moment of our lives.

WE DO NOT NEED MORE CONFIDENCE BECAUSE WE CAN PERFORM EVEN WHEN WE DO NOT THINK WE CAN

The biggest issue with confidence comes when we believe that we need it and that something is wrong when we do not have it. There is more to performing than feeling good. Being caught up in trying to be more confident gets in the way of how capable we actually are even when we do not feel it.

Whilst confidence is a great feeling to have, there is nothing that we actually *need* it for. The only thing that stops us doing what we would do when we feel confident is listening to insecure thoughts. Instead of listening to those thoughts, we can perform anyway. We can ask somebody a question or watch the ball and hit it, regardless of how we are feeling.

Our level of confidence projects a virtual reality of how we think the game will play out. If we are high on confidence we *think* it will go smoothly, but if we are low on confidence, we *think* it will go badly. Neither is objectively true. We will find out how capable we really are when we 'just play' despite any doubts. It does not matter whether we think we can or we think we cannot, we just have to do it and find out.

Everybody has had occasions when they have felt very low in confidence but found a way to perform to a high level. Equally, everybody has had times when they felt 'a million dollars' and it seemed inevitable that we were going to succeed but we did not (e.g. a batsman who is feeling great, convinced that they are going to score a hundred as they walk out to bat, but swings the bat towards their first ball, edges it and is caught!).

Athletes often say, "I didn't think I could win today" and then they do. This is because their ability to perform is not impaired by the doubtful thoughts they are having unless they believe them to be true. As we realise that our performances are not reliant on having to feel confident, we automatically let go of the insecure thinking that causes a prolonged feeling of low confidence. It stops making sense to keep replaying, in our minds, all the thinking that is making us feel low when we realise that it cannot actually influence the outcome.

Feeling confident is great, but there is nothing wrong with being low in confidence. It is simply a reflection of the ever-changing and fluctuating thinking we have in the moment. We cannot control how we will feel when we walk out onto the pitch, but we can always trust that deeper sense of *knowing* what to do even when we do not feel like it. We are still the same player when we are feeling low just as when we are feeling on top of our game. Our capabilities are intact.

Once we *know* we are OK, the transient thoughts that trick us that we are not suddenly have a lot less appeal. We become OK in times of low confidence because we *know* there is more to us than how we feel in that moment. This is the essence of being comfortable feeling uncomfortable. Sometimes playing the game feels effortless and sometimes it feels far from it, but no matter what thoughts are passing through our minds, when we *know* what to do we can do it because we are still as good an athlete whether we feel confident or not.

RESILIENCE

Resilience is seeing the situations we are in, and our successes and failures, for what they are. This allows us to learn and move on without struggling or suffering.

RESILIENCE IS INNATE

Everybody is born with all the resilience they need to overcome the events that take place on and off the field. We may all have different personalities, perspectives, skills and abilities, but we all born resilient. All we need is to know it.

There is no better example than a child learning to walk. Every child 'fails' more while learning to walk than they are likely to at any other task over the rest of their lifetime. Nothing shakes them off their course. They pass no judgement on their inability to succeed. They keep going, again and again until they are able to walk. They fail until they succeed. Children also display their innate resilience when they move on from feeling upset without having to do anything about it. One minute they are having a tantrum and the next they are playing and having fun.

The difference between the simplicity of the resilience displayed by children and how we respond in later years is not the difficulty of the task, but the amount of thinking that gets in the way. We think ourselves out of our resilience by coming up with, and believing, reasons why something cannot be done.

We are all designed to be resilient. Everybody's mind is built to self-correct, to flow from a low state to a high state of its own accord. The mind clears thought just as the rest of our vital organs function without us having to think about it. The resilience of our mind is only suppressed when it is full of misunderstandings about how our experience is created.

We can get over anything when we know what it is we have to get over. Resilience is moving past, or taking less to heart, the stories we tell ourselves about what the events that take place mean. Once an event has happened, it exists only in our thinking. We have the capacity to see that and move on, no matter how hard it may feel. How we respond to challenging circumstances reveals the degree to which we understand how resilient we are or how thought gets in the way. People will make mistakes and teams will lose, but our capacity for resilience always remains exactly the same – infinite.

NOBODY IS INHERENTLY MENTALLY TOUGHER THAN ANYBODY ELSE

Everybody is born with the same capacity for mental strength and resilience, but some people intuitively realise and retain it more than others. Our resilience can only be lost through the habits, beliefs and fears we collect through our thinking. We learn to trust "can't", "don't", or "shouldn't" thoughts more than our innate capability to overcome them.

Real mental strength comes from inside. It is not something that has to be learned, built or shown off; only understood. Mental strength does not come from what we have – e.g. power or status – or from what we have done, nor do we have to act tough to be resilient. It is understanding that we will feel low at times, but that it is thought and it is perfectly OK. There is nothing we have to do about it. No matter how we act, or what we think or feel, resilience is a part of who we are.

We do not have to get over the events that take place (e.g. making a mistake or getting dropped from the team). We always, and only, move on when our perception about the event shifts. This can happen in an instant. If we never feel ready to move on it is because of all the thinking (e.g. how it is not fair or how we wish we could have done it differently) we are holding onto. When all the thinking that keeps us where we are is released, we move on with the learning or the appreciation of what the experience provided, rather than fight against what it is not. Our experiences can teach us how resilient we really are, even if we would have preferred it to have played out another way.

This does not mean it is easy. Painful thinking creates painful feelings, and when we care about something it makes sense to think about it a lot. We all get caught in low thoughts and feelings to some extent. When we are in the midst of it, the solution looks far off. However, further analysis and rumination on our situation, or attempting to control or fix how we feel, only serves to prolong our low state of mind and gets in the way of our innate resilience.

There is nothing to do, or to try, to be mentally tougher. It happens naturally when we realise it was already there before all our beliefs and interpretations became layered on top. Resilience is a case of letting go of, or moving through, what appears to get in the way, rather than having to think or behave in a certain way.

WE RESPOND HOW WE RESPOND AND WE CAN FORGIVE OURSELVES FOR THAT

It is OK to 'lose it', be frustrated, disappointed or angry. It is OK to not feel OK. It is OK to be moody. It is OK not to have it together at any moment. We do not need to fight negative thoughts. Feeling low is not anyone's fault. We are human and should not attempt to be an emotionless robot.

We cannot control what our next thought (and therefore, feeling) is going to be. If it is a judgmental or upsetting thought, then that is what it is. Just because we have that thought, it does not mean we have to believe it, ruminate about it or act on it (although we may do all three and that is OK too).

Everybody reacts differently to bad days; the most resilient people do not take it personally – they learn from it and move on. Being resilient does not mean that we do not feel despondent when we lose, cry when we are upset, lash out when we are feeling angry, sulk when we are disappointed or beat ourselves up when we make a mistake. Outside-in illusions look compelling for everyone at times.

Resilience is subsequently seeing that those emotions were coming only from the stories we are telling ourselves about what the game means or how we wanted it to work out. There is nothing external to us that can make us feel upset, angry or disappointed. Only getting lost in our thinking about how the world should be can do that. It does not make us an angry or judgmental type of person except for that moment where we experienced an angry or judgmental thought and believed it.

While we can take performing very seriously, we can also have a lot of fun. Sometimes we can dwell on what has happened for hours, but once we have learnt from the experience, playing it over and over in our minds again has very little benefit. Our interpretation of the world can be filled with disappointment if we hold on to those thoughts long enough. When we let go of those thoughts it can be filled with calm, learning and enjoyment, even when we are not at our best.

At times, we are going to feel low even when we have 'smashed it out of the park'. At other times, we can have a nightmare of a performance and feel OK with it. When we know this, we see that we are OK no matter how we are feeling. While the situations that we are in will change, our experience is never dependent on them. We are fundamentally OK no matter what goes on in the game. With that understanding, we will see how we can make the best of the situation with our own intelligence and common-sense.

We do not have to pretend that we did not make a mistake or that it did not annoy us. The more understand the true nature of resilience, the way that we react to events shifts in ways that reflect that understanding. Our perspective on what happens broadens as we understand where our experience is coming from.

The clearer we are seeing it, the quicker and more effectively we pick ourselves up, make amends if we need to and get back to what we are here to do – love, laugh, lose ourselves in the moment and make a difference. We will feel what we feel, we will act how we act, but as we open up to how the human experience flows through us from the inside-out we become more of what we already are – resilient.

RESILIENCE IS SEEING THE SITUATION AS IT IS

We think that our progress will be straight-forward. It seems logical that B will follow A and C will swiftly occur thereafter. However, our journeys and our learning often turn out to be far more random and unpredictable. No-one ever reaches the top in a totally linear progression. Even Michael Jordan, the greatest basketballer of all-time, was dropped from his high school team.

Every great athlete has had their difficulties and hurdles to overcome, from getting dropped or being injured to performances not matching up to expectations, to having to hear the criticism of the media or fans. Those that overcome all of these issues do not possess any capacity for dealing with it that everyone else does not. They are normal people who have performed, learned and improved their abilities through the challenges they have encountered, because they utilised the capacity to overcome that is innate in all of us.

Setbacks are a perception or interpretation. The idea of 'failure' is an illusion made of thought – what seems like a failure to one person, does not to another. It is a concept that we are continually making up and then believing in. What feels like failure to us one day, does not the next. One person's setback is 'water off a duck's back' to another.

Problems and setbacks appear differently in different states of mind. In a low mood a situation looks fatal; in a higher state of mind, we see the opportunity. We can see any experience from an infinite number of viewpoints. What looks like a problem from one perspective might be a blessing or a solution from another. A problem is only a problem when we are not seeing the situation as it is. It is resistance to reality that creates psychological suffering, not the actual situation or incident itself.

"Whatever the present moment contains, accept as if you had chosen it. Always work with it, not against it."

—Eckhart Tolle (Philosopher).

Defeats say absolutely nothing about who we are, although they might say plenty about the skills that we have and what we can improve. Defeats are defeats. The game is one experience after another. When we perceive adversity, a setback or a problem then that is just one way of looking at the situation. There is nothing wrong with looking at it that way, as we all will do at times. However, the truth is that we have had an experience and then loaded it with meaning (good, bad or indifferent) through our thinking.

The more strongly we believe that winning is critical, the more psychological discomfort we experience when we lose or fail. If we build a sense of identity in our minds that depends upon how well we are doing then we will become habitually engaged in making excuses or trying to rationalise why we have lost or were not as good as we could have been. This is a defence mechanism to protect that false sense of ourselves.

Instead of collecting judgements about ourselves and creating stories about what the defeat means, our perspective shifts when we see that a defeat is not a drama and we can laugh at the discomfort a thought about losing can cause to our ego. Without losing there would be no wins or successes worth celebrating. Therefore, while we are never likely to enjoy losing, we can always be OK with it.

It is impossible to avoid making mistakes or bumping into obstacles. They are inevitable for us all. Whatever happens, happens. Some of it we will enjoy and other elements, we will not. However, until we appreciate the experience for what it is, we are so busy clinging to our story about who we think we are or worrying about the past or planning a tomorrow that might not come that we forget our strength and resilience to deal with the situation as it is right now. Nobody wants to get it wrong. However, what we want is not always what we need. A loss might seem like a 'failure', but in a year's time it might seem like a gift if we have learned from it.

LEARNING FROM OUR EXPERIENCES COMES FROM UNDERSTANDING THEM

Our experiences have no inherent power. Only our state of mind in the moment determines our perception of an experience as good or bad, useful or a waste of time. If we had a different thought at the time, we would feel differently about it.

We may learn from an experience in an instant or later with time and perspective ("I hated it at the time, but I am much better for it now") or not learn at all. Our openness to learning determines what we see and what we will do next. The more we understand that a circumstance cannot control how we feel, the less sense it makes to give attention to our negative interpretations of the game. From a perspective of clarity, we have room to take a next step that is helpful and productive.

The best players are constantly evolving by improving their skills and the depth of their game understanding, whilst remaining true to their strengths. We have to be able to see our game as it is – both its strengths and weaknesses – and have the desire to learn, otherwise we will do what we have always done because we are used to it (our comfort zone).

Knowing what we need to work on in training to become a better performer, regardless of whether we are knocking it out the park or missing the ball altogether, helps to avoid a blind search of how and when to improve. Otherwise, a sequence of defeats or 'poor form' can send athletes on a wild goose chase to fix a game that might not need fixing.

Sometimes when our results drop, we try to change our game in an attempt to feel better. It makes us feel that we are doing something productive. However, this is fundamentally different to *knowing* the areas of our game we are working on to become a better player, regardless of recent results. The feeling of desperation and the search for a quick fix often only takes us further away from what we are looking for. This search for a quick fix is a coping strategy to deal with the thinking we have about our results. This only serves to mess with our game more as we lose sight of seeing our game as it truly is.

Everybody feels frustrated when the gap between how good they currently are and how good they want to be (or think they should be) looks distant. However, this is only an interpretation. Whether our game needs changing or not, when our mood shifts our problems look different. In a better mood, with more perspective, the gap between where we are and the player we want to be looks like an exciting challenge. Then common-sense solutions seem to occur to us as we are having fun exploring how to close the gap.

The best learning is our own learning. An experience or a piece of advice cannot, on its own, teach us anything. We only learn through insight. This is a meaningful, but almost effortless, change that enables us to see or do something differently than before. It occurs as we instinctively experience a fresh thought or perspective about the experience.

This is why some people learn from their experiences and other people do not – some people get so lost in their habitual thinking that they never have the mental space to see something new. There comes a point when almost all the players at a certain level are working equally as hard to be the best player they can be. At this point, the difference lies in getting more out of that time, rather than grinding ourselves into the ground.

Improvement in our abilities may be preceded by hundreds of hours of practice, it may be a hundred different experiences all connecting into one insight about how to move or play better. Alternatively, it might be a single thought that randomly occurs to us when we are doing something completely different.

The moments when our game seems to intuitively 'click into place' are more likely to occur when we are curious about how to get better and take enjoyment in playing the game. We get in our own way when our minds are full of judgmental thinking about how we are not good enough or how we cannot get our bodies to make the technical changes that we want.

All our experiences, successes and failures, are an opening to our innate capacity for learning. However, if we do not see it, we are likely to collide with all our thinking about how bad the situation is or how badly we performed. If we do not get wrapped up in our interpretation, our capacity to see things as they are and to learn is always intact.

"I've gone through the worst loss of my career, in the most public eye that golf has. Everything I've gone through, both good and bad, is advantageous for me. If I win tomorrow, I'll still be learning."

—Jordan Speith (Golf – on the eve of winning the 2016 Open, having lost a 5 shot lead on the last day at the 2015 Masters).

RESILIENCE IS BEING ABLE TO LAUGH AND CARRY ON EVEN WHEN IT HURTS

Even in the most difficult of situations, it pays not to be too serious. We can be whole-heartedly committed and still enjoy ourselves, even when we want to play our best. Having fun does not mean we are being careless. When we get very serious about the game and we get lost in our thinking about what could go wrong, we tense up and play as if it is life and death. It usually helps to see the lighter side of any situation.

Optimism is the natural result of realising our ceaseless capacity for resilience. It is inevitable that we are more optimistic and enjoy the moment more when we know that it is in-built in us to overcome all of life's circumstances. It is possible to care deeply about our performance and to give it everything, yet still walk off at the end of the day and smile at what has happened – whether it exceeded expectations, went to plan or not. A way of looking on the bright side, and taking the learning from it, always exists even if it does not feel that way in the immediate aftermath of a game.

When our teammates are going through a tough time, the most helpful thing we can do is to be ourselves and be understanding, with the knowledge that the difficult time is not the cause of our emotions, no matter how much it looks that way in the moment. This demonstrates to them how resilience is in their nature just as it is in ours.

Being resilient is not giving up when our thoughts and feelings are telling us to quit, that it is not worth it, or that we should save our effort. Getting a 'second wind' is seeing these thoughts for what they are and continuing on regardless. Long-distance runners report the 'second wind' effect, where their tiredness increases up to a certain point until it suddenly disappears and they feel fresh again.

We so rarely push through that point of fatigue or disappointment that we do not see potential that exists beyond it. The ability to continue onwards even when we do not feel like it, lies in the power of the second wind and the second wind starts when we see the transient, illusory nature of the thoughts that tell us that we cannot.

> *"Most people never run far enough on their first wind to find out they've got a second. Give your dreams all you've got and you'll be amazed at the energy that comes out of you."*
>
> *—William James (a founder of the science of Psychology).*

MOTIVATION

"Money is not a motivating factor. Money doesn't thrill me or make me play better just because there are benefits to being wealthy. I'm just happy with a ball at my feet. My motivation comes from playing the game I love. If I wasn't paid to be a professional footballer I would willingly play for nothing."

—Lionel Messi (Football – 8 La Liga titles & 4 Champions League titles with Barcelona)

WE ARE BORN MOTIVATED TO DO THINGS BECAUSE THEY ARE ENJOYABLE, OR TO SEE WHAT WE ARE CAPABLE OF OR BECAUSE THEY JUST MAKE SENSE

Intrinsic motivation is doing something because simply doing it is its own reward. A child does not have to be incentivised to learn how to walk. Children set about accomplishing it because it intuitively makes sense to them. Extrinsic motivation is when we do things for the rewards, such as results, money or the approval of others. We learn to be motivated by things outside of us, as we are conditioned by the society around us of their value. They are concepts that society has made up and we end up believing that we need them. Money, fame and recognition can be great, but a blind pursuit of them can end in deep dissatisfaction even when they are acquired.

Money, for example, is an extremely useful tool but it is not a source of happiness no matter how much it can look that way. There are plenty of people who have almost nothing who are far more satisfied and have a far richer experience of life than people who seemingly have everything we could wish for. If we believe we are motivated by money, or anything else outside of us, we have bought into the illusion that something outside of us can create how we feel. It is a habit of thinking that we pick up if we believe it to be true. Like all habits, it can be harmless, or it can be destructive, but as we wake up to it then it lessens its hold.

An athlete who becomes predominantly motivated by external rewards can be equally or more successful at a game than someone who is intrinsically motivated to do the same task. However, their experience of it will be very different. For someone who has bought into an illusion of needing extrinsic rewards, what started as a game that they played for enjoyment can become a grind or a battle. It becomes about achieving whichever illusion they have been seduced by and the fun can disappear almost entirely.

Players connected with their innate, intrinsic motivation (which appears as a love of the game) keep playing and performing as long as they are enjoying it and it feels right. All the external rewards then look after themselves, an almost effortless by-product of working at what they love.

Enjoying external rewards can be great, but it is not a fundamental part of our nature in the way that intrinsic motivation is. In a hundred years' time, the extrinsic rewards we value may be completely different. They change as people's thinking changes. We can have the best of both when we know which is true and which is an illusion. We get into trouble when we lose ourselves in the extrinsic illusion and go from being able to enjoy the simplest of activities to our mind never being satisfied, as it continually searches for bigger and better activities or rewards. In that process we unintentionally remove the fun from playing a game.

WE LOSE MOTIVATION WHEN WE GET LOST IN OUR THINKING

Whether it is a low mood or recurring thoughts about how we are not good enough or it feels like we want it too badly, a loss of motivation is always caused by thought. As thought fluctuates through high moods and lower ones, it is inevitable that we will all experience drops in motivation at times. However, when we understand the innate nature of motivation it becomes clearer to see when we are caught in a temporary, illusory perspective or we have been inspired to take a different route.

When our motivation drops, and we take that seriously, then our attitude, body language and behaviours will follow suit. We would all love to have a great attitude all the time, but our perspective constantly shifts with the thinking we are having. It often seems like it is the game or our performances that cause a loss of motivation. However, it is impossible to enjoy the game when we are busy comparing our performances to the past or judging ourselves by the player we *think* we should be.

A loss of motivation is a temporary collection of thinking in a temporary perspective that makes our efforts feel pointless. It becomes a habit if we take these thoughts in a low state of mind to heart so much that we start building a sense of identity around them. Then how we act will reflect that negativity. Therefore, disengaged body language and disruptive behaviours are simply a reflection of having taken that feeling, and the thinking causing it, seriously. However, if we see it is only temporary, and illusory, then its hold over us will not last for long.

"Everybody is doing the best they can, given the thinking they have that looks real to them."

—Sydney Banks (Philosopher).

When we fixate on external rewards as a source of motivation, then whilst our ability to achieve goals might not be impaired, our capacity to enjoy them will be. Peace of mind becomes fleeting as we develop patterns of thinking that mean that as soon as we have ticked off one accomplishment, we start on the next.

The outside-in illusion can become so compelling that we override enjoyment in the pursuit of achievement When we forget that we are playing a game, we stop playing the game itself and start using our performances to validate an illusory sense of identity and self-worth. There is nothing wrong with becoming successful by any conventional measure, but we do not have to be trapped by it. We can define success as we want to or simply play the game as it comes, without any expectations at all.

We all have an inner sense of knowing about what is a fun or worthy use of our time and endeavour. Trusting our intuition can lead us to accomplish all sorts of things we did not even consider, or think were possible. When thought causing a loss of motivation passes, we reconnect with our innate source of drive and enthusiasm. Enjoying the moment, regardless of what we are doing or where we are, is natural. It happens every time our mind clears and we relax into that feeling.

TRYING TO MOTIVATE OURSELVES OR WAITING TO FEEL MOTIVATED ONLY GETS IN THE WAY

It can feel as if we need to be in a certain frame of mind to do certain things, but this is a trick of the mind. When we are in a low state of mind, everything can feel arduous or we think that we are not ready. These are temporary illusions. If we *know* what must be done – e.g. attend training, do an extra gym session – then we know we can do it whether we feel like it or not. The more we throw ourselves into what we are doing, no matter how we are feeling, the more we get back. As we lose ourselves in the game, the more enjoyment we experience.

Motivation cannot be sustainably forced or created, neither by ourselves nor by other people. Trying to be motivated or taking on someone else's view of motivation only creates more thinking. Sometimes we all need the odd nudge or even a proverbial kick up the backside, because we get caught up in our thinking. However, motivational speeches have diminishing returns. They might knock people out of their thinking once in a while, but we quickly tire of them because they make the mistake of assuming that something on the outside can create a sustainable feeling of motivation on the inside.

When our understanding of where our feelings are coming from in the moment rises, our behaviours reflect that deeper understanding. During the times when our understanding drops and we fall into the outside-in illusion, we behave differently, often in a less productive way (e.g. if it appears as though our coach is making us feel angry it might make sense to rebel against them and become disruptive). It is not possible for us to directly get other people to change, nor is it possible for us to simply click our fingers and have a completely different perspective and ways of operating for ourselves. When we see things differently (i.e. have a change of heart for ourselves), it intuitively and effortlessly stops making sense to behave the way we did previously.

A leader's role is help their team see how sustained motivation comes from within – from the intelligence that *knows* what to do even when we do not feel like it, from the feeling of inspiration that comes from having a clear mind. When we understand how the mind works, we all act with more common-sense. Therefore, more collective understanding means we need less intervention and control to govern behaviour. We see that as the mind naturally self-corrects, behaviours do too.

When we understand the cause of our feelings, how motivated we feel starts to matter less. Whether we are momentarily having positive or negative thinking, we are free to get on with what we need to regardless. If we did not listen to the thoughts that pop into our head, we would not just stand there lost. We would automatically do whatever it is we are going to do on instinct, based on what we *know* is the next (or right) thing to do. This deep motivating force is more powerful, sustainable and enjoyable than when we buy into false ideas of what we need in life to motivate ourselves.

COMMITTING TO BEING THE BEST WE CAN BE DOES NOT MEAN WE HAVE TO TAKE OURSELVES SERIOUSLY

Commitment provides clarity. It binds us to what we are doing despite all the ups and downs, insecurities and doubters. It frees us from the devices of our own mind. When we commit fully to something, alternative ideas stop making sense and our attention falls into the moment. Commitment brings a freedom from everything else that could be happening.

When we are not committed and spend half the time thinking of doing our best and half considering an alternative use of our time, we suffer the reality of being in neither place. For example, when we are at training but are thinking about exams, or at a match and thinking about the consequences, we are not fully in one place or the other. The more we commit to the present moment, to the game and to enjoying ourselves, we become immersed in it so that even the most mundane of activities becomes fulfilling.

Because we want to do well, it can become easy to confuse commitment with taking ourselves seriously. Commitment creates space for our natural focus, effort and enjoyment. It is giving it our best shot however it plays out. Being committed enables athletes to compete to the fullest of their abilities, even in what might seem to be a hopeless situation, without having to think twice about it. Taking it seriously is what we do when we believe our results determine who we are. When we take ourselves seriously we can end up playing the game as if our life depends on it, often leading to tensing up and limiting the risks and opportunities we take.

When we take ourselves seriously we take all the fun out of what we do. We forget that we are playing a game and begin to lose our natural motivation. Our commitment and enjoyment wavers less when we are playing for the love of the game and our own internal challenge, rather than trying to prove or protect our ego's ideas about how good we are or must be. Sport is about pushing the boundaries of what we can do, solving problems and competing to find our limits. However, many of us fall into habits of thinking that turn playing sport into a mechanism that creates a false sense of identity about who we are depending on whether we do well or not.

We diminish our connection to the game with the stories we tell ourselves about what it means, rather than enjoying the game for what it is. We tell ourselves we have to be *this* good or that we will only be happy when we get to *this* level. We collect thinking about how well we must do – sometimes from others – and unwittingly use it against ourselves to create a less enjoyable and less engaged experience. As we create higher expectations, set goals and take the objective 'making it' more and more seriously, the game can become unrecognisable to the connection we felt when we fell in love with it.

Our performances are only as important as we think they are. We can try our best and play for fun regardless of the level we are at. Having fun does not mean we are not committed. When we play sport for the games that they are, rather than believing that they are a measure of us as a person, they bring out the best in us. We become lost in the moment and feel a sense of freedom and connection, whilst finding solutions and being creative. It is possible to have fun and play brilliantly. Performance does not have to be a grind.

As we become more committed, we become more connected with what we are doing. We become less afraid of what might happen or what others will think and instead play 'full out' for the enjoyment of it. Giving it everything to win is brilliant, but we do not have to take it personally if we lose – the game might be gone, but we are still OK.

RECONNECTING WITH OUR LOVE OF THE GAME

When we started playing sport we did not play it to achieve a certain target or to make ourselves look good, we played it because it was fun and we enjoyed ourselves. That happened because we were fully immersed in and energised by playing the game. That is our natural approach to sport and life itself.

The more we have a good time and give it our best effort, the more effortlessly results follow. We drop unhelpful habits of thinking that create feelings of pressure when we remember that enjoyment is the reason for playing in the first place. When it looks like we are motivated by things other than enjoyment and the love of the game, it is worth considering whether those ideas are helping or hindering our performances.

Almost everyone falls in love with their sport through some very simple experiences. This might be playing in the back garden with family, the simple pleasure of striking the ball cleanly or enjoying the opportunity to run about and have fun. Some of the most competitive games of sport ever played have been battled out by children out in the backyard. The reason they are so enjoyable is that you can give it everything, and if it does not come off, you know that it does not say anything about you as a human being. If you are out first ball or miss an open goal, then it is all a part of the game. Children do not create stories about backyard games that they use to define themselves as a person. This is a habit we innocently, but unhelpfully, fall into as we get older.

We all have preferences depending on the thinking we have and what we take seriously. There are games, weather, people, holidays and events we prefer to others. However, our preferences are not written in stone. We might hate a part of the game or training at one point, and then end up enjoying it further down the line. The more we commit to what we are doing, the less appealing ruminating on thoughts about alternatives or frustration becomes. Enjoyment and engagement are key to getting the most out of whatever we are doing, whether it is our 'preference' or not.

We are most productive when we are doing what we love, simply because we love doing it. Worrying about our own or others' expectations seems pointless when we are doing what we love. When we fall out of our thinking and into the moment, we can play our best game without even realising how we are doing it. It is almost as if we have no time to even consider the prospect of pressure. We are so aware of the game, that paying attention to anything else (including how we are feeling about the game or the consequences) simply makes no sense.

We can feel incredibly motivated to do the simplest activities in the world (e.g. a child playing in the sandpit) or the most complex and challenging situations (e.g. sport at the highest level). They actually have nothing to do with the task and everything to do with our state of mind whilst we are doing them. Ultimately our love of the game is not coming from the game itself, it is coming from us. Love is a state of mind; a feeling that flows through us.

The game cannot create that feeling of connection, but as all of our thinking drops away, we are connected in the moment. We can fall into this naturally motivated, immersed, energised state of flow doing anything. We reconnect to our love of the game by dropping all the misunderstandings that get in the way of what is already there, so that our enjoyment is not contingent on certain conditions or having to be 'this good', but we simply play the game for what it is.

Playing sport provides a never-ending sequence of challenges to address and opportunities to enjoy the ups and downs of competition as our limits are stretched and we become more skilled. This becomes simpler when we do the one thing that we can do right now to progress, because it feels right, without worrying what will happen if it goes wrong. Playing the game is broken down to one opportunity after another to play and to learn. As we understand our innate nature and the game more clearly, knowing when to act becomes intuitive so that it seems common-sense whether to push on or to ease off.

When we play the game because we love it, we automatically experience and demonstrate resilience, determination, perspective and have fun doing it. The love of the game drives sustainable effort that enables us to go the extra mile without hassle and allows us to absorb the rough times, as well as enjoy the good times, because we are playing for more than results.

"Sometimes you're just happy playing. Some people, unfortunately, don't understand that it's okay just to play tennis and enjoy it. They always think you have to win everything, it always needs to be a success story, and if it's

not, obviously, what is the point? Maybe you have to go back and think, why have I started playing tennis? Because I just like it. It's actually sort of a dream hobby that became somewhat of a job. Some people just don't get that, ever."

—Roger Federer (Tennis – 20 'Grand Slam' titles).

PERFORMANCE

"There are some days you feel really good and other days not so much, but you accept every day is going to be different. You want everything to be perfect, but it doesn't really happen like that, so it's being okay with that. Ultimately just trying to adapt each day is quite important. Although it can be frustrating at times, it is a challenge and something you want to allow into your game."
—Kane Williamson (New Zealand Cricket Captain)

PERFORMING HOWEVER WE ARE FEELING

Understanding that pressure does not come from outside us – i.e. the difficulty or importance of the situation, the consequences or the opinions of others – does not make us immune from feeling it from time to time. Thought is continually forming and flowing through everybody.

In the moments when we get caught up in the feelings that are passing through our minds, it really feels as if we are unable to perform. Thoughts that suggest "you're not good enough" appear both true and inhibiting. However, whilst our thoughts and feelings create our experience of the game, they are powerless to prevent us from performing despite how we feel, unless we believe otherwise.

THERE IS NO OPTIMUM OR NECESSARY STATE OF MIND THAT WE NEED TO BE IN TO PERFORM

We can still hit, kick, catch and throw regardless of how under pressure we feel. It is only that in a lower state of mind it really feels as if we can't! The more we realise our abilities can shine independent of what we are thinking or feeling, the more they do. When we are in a lower state of mind, it feels tough and tricky and in a higher state of mind it feels free and easy, but our capacity to perform remains exactly the same.

There is nothing more limiting than believing that there is a state of mind that is required for us to be at our best. It becomes self-fulfilling as we make our ability to perform contingent on the occasions when thought shifts one way and not another. If we believe that there is a certain way that we should feel, we do more thinking in an attempt to find this state or fix our current state of mind. This only serves to make us feel more agitated. Whenever we experience an uncomfortable feeling we might assume that it means we cannot perform to our potential. However, it is only when we believe that to be true that it becomes exactly what happens.

We have an infinite, innate, instinctive intelligence that enables us to perform. This intelligence is a constant, behind the transient thoughts and emotions that pass through our minds. How we are feeling on the sports field stops being a problem when we wake up to the truth that we are 'good to go' no matter how we are feeling. We can just go out and play. If we are feeling out of rhythm or we make a mistake, there is nothing to think or worry about. We can just keep playing because, deep down, we already know what to do.

As a result of this instinctive intelligence, we are no more capable or incapable of making a hundred in cricket or scoring a penalty kick, whether we are in the zone or feeling nervous. We are always capable of making the best of whatever state of mind we are in to perform our skills and find a way to succeed. When we have less on our minds, we get results with less effort. Yet when we have more on our minds, we are still the same player with the same ability – it just feels as if we are not. Playing with freedom is realising there is not a set of conditions (e.g. a certain state of mind) that we need in order to play the way that feels right to us.

The illusion of 'needing' pressure to perform is a thought that suggests that without the feeling of being 'up for it', we will not be able to play our best. Sometimes when people experience pressure and are successful under that feeling they assume that, although it is not pleasant, they need to feel under stress to perform to their highest level. From that misunderstanding, they begin to fall into habits of thinking that make them feel 'on edge' more and more of the time. However, feeling under pressure is never required for high performance.

The feeling of pressure may come and go, but we do not need to create more of any feeling to be able to play our best, despite how it often it can look that way. The correlation between experiencing pressure and being able or unable to perform is just that, it is not causation. Pressure cannot cause high performance, but neither can it inhibit our performances unless we believe it can.

OUR EMOTIONS CANNOT DISRUPT OUR ABILITY TO PERFORM

We are going to experience every possible emotion whilst playing sport and that is absolutely fine. Feelings and emotions are inherently neutral – we determine whether they are 'positive' or 'negative'. There are times when feeling upset, angry and aggressive on the field are the most beneficial emotions we can experience. Only when we get lost in them and attribute the cause of the feeling to something other than thought, do they become destructive to what we are trying to achieve.

Nobody can control what their next thought is going to be. Emotions are a product of thought which moves to its own rhythm. The more we see where our emotions are coming from, the more they regulate themselves to what we need in the moment. When we understand that the root of panic or impatience is thoughts that cause psychological disturbance, we let go of the thinking just as we would take our hands off a hot stove that is causing a physical disturbance.

Our decisions and responses in a game are always the result of how we see the situation at that point of time. We always do what makes sense given the thinking we have. Our response is never directly caused by what has happened – e.g. a wrong decision from the umpire, abuse from the crowd or losing the game. It is always dependent on our interpretation of the situation. That interpretation is always a result of the intuitive understanding of the cause of how we are feeling that we have in that moment. This level of understanding is continually rising and falling. If our level of understanding of where our feelings are coming from is low in that moment, then we are more likely to lash out, be disrespectful or get thrown off our game.

There are times when it looks like we can control the thoughts and emotions running through our heads. In reality, it is that another thought has occurred to us or our attention has gone in a different direction and it no longer makes sense to hold onto the thinking we just had. If our intuitive understanding of the cause of our feelings is high, the thought "calm down" or "just keep playing" may occur to us during an intense part of play. However, when we do not see where the feeling is coming from, then a very different thought is likely to look compelling.

Either way, we do not need to worry about 'getting a grip' of our emotions. They are energy passing through us – we are still OK – and, when we stop adding more thinking by trying to control our emotions, we have space to see the situation with more clarity. Although our feelings appear to be coming from what is going on in the game, they are only ever a direct feedback loop for what we are thinking in that moment.

We feel angry when we have angry thinking going on inside our heads. It is impossible for someone or something to directly make us feel angry. As we see that anger and frustration comes from the gap between how we *think* things should be and how they are in reality, engaging with our angry thinking about the situation begins to lose its appeal. A refereeing decision cannot make us feel frustrated, playing in new conditions cannot make it feel impossible and failing cannot make us feel like a failure. When we see that, positive rather than destructive behaviours emerge.

We can have a thought or feeling without acting on it. Nobody reacts to all their thinking. Simply experiencing an emotion cannot cause our behaviour. It is how we relate or react to it in the moment. The more we see where our feelings are coming from, the less sense it makes to act on the thinking we have in our low moments. If we 'lose it', then we can see that it was because we lost our bearings on where our feelings were coming from at that time. We do not need to think ourselves even further away by 'beating ourselves up' about it – everyone becomes lost in their thinking from time-to-time.

We are the same player that we were immediately before experiencing the feeling and we will still be the same player once the feeling has passed. Our experience may be changing, but our ability is a constant. Because of that, in any moment, we are always able to play to our potential and make match-winning contributions.

> *"I can't just be ice, it becomes horribly boring. I need the fire, the excitement, the passion, the whole rollercoaster."*
>
> *—Roger Federer.*

A FOOTBALLER CAN BE STANDING OVER A PENALTY IN A WORLD CUP FINAL UTTERLY CONVINCED THAT THEY ARE GOING TO MISS AND THEN STEP UP AND SCORE

Just because we think something is going to happen does not mean that it will. This explains why life is full of 'that was better than I thought it was going to be' experiences. When the footballer steps up it does not matter what they are thinking. They do not have to stop the thinking that's going on. All they have to do is step up and kick the ball towards the goal.

There is little point in trying to tell ourselves "I'm going to score" (although that thought might naturally appear anyway) or that we are great, because our instincts already know how to do it. In a low state of mind, it might feel temporarily reassuring, but the insecure feelings we are trying to talk our way away from are just as temporary and transient as those that we try to replace them with. This only serves to get in the way of the mind's natural design. When thought changes, we will feel positive with no effort or willpower whatsoever. Even when we are not feeling confident, we can still kick the ball into the goal.

Most players perform well when they are in a state of mind that feels like 'the zone'. The best players are those that understand that feeling off their game is not a major problem. They are still able to find a way to be effective. They make use of the tools that they have in the 'kit-bag' of their skills and abilities on that particular day, rather being concerned about how their performance is not flowing. They are comfortable feeling uncomfortable and always look to make the most of the situation.

Some athletes find that they play to their best level in training or in the backyard but find it hard to transfer that level of performance into competitive matches. These players are carrying more thinking about the illusions of the game's importance or difficulty, the consequences or people's judgements, into the game, and believing it. This thinking gets in the way of the player that they were yesterday at training when they played with freedom and everything came off. We do not have the choice about how we feel in the middle of the game, but we do have the capacity to understand where the feeling is coming from and still play our best in the situation we find ourselves in.

We have a natural propensity to excel no matter what we are thinking or feeling. Our performances are only limited by our state of mind to the degree that we believe that our state of mind can affect our performance. The more we understand that the relationship between our state of mind and performance is neutral – we do not have to be in any state of mind to perform and that we cannot control our state of mind – the less it bothers us what is on our mind and, in turn, our potential to perform rises. The more we understand this, the more peak performance can flow naturally of its own accord.

"Sometimes you're looking to play perfect tennis but it's not going to happen all the time and you have to accept it."

—Andy Murray (3 Tennis 'Grand Slams' and Olympic Gold Medallist).

CONCENTRATION IS FAR MORE NATURAL AND ACCESSIBLE THAN WE MIGHT THINK

'The zone' is an effortless, instinctive state of deep concentration, where our performance flows. It is a naturally occurring state of awareness where everything other than the game falls away. Thoughts pass through our minds so fluently that we barely notice them. Clarity, intuition, effort and focus all merge together so that every movement and each action follows on seamlessly from the last. We feel as if we can keep going forever as our energy levels do not significantly deplete despite the amount of effort that appears to be going into the performance.

In 'the zone' we find higher and higher levels of performance without having to force it. We are simply immersed in the game and lose all sense of self-consciousness so that all insecurity about the consequences falls away. We are completely 'in the moment' despite making no effort to be. We do things that we did not even know we were capable of and perform to a level that we did not even know existed. The game can feel as if it is in slow motion, as our mind is so attuned to what is relevant (e.g. the ball, the opponent) and nothing else seems to matter (e.g. analysis of the past or worries about the future).

This state can feel like an out-of-body experience, where creativity and instinctive play emerge naturally. Due to being in a deep state of concentration, after the game it can feel hard to explain how and what we did to play so well because everything seemed to be taking place of its own accord. In this instinctive state we are fully aware of what we are doing, but it is hard to claim that we deserve the credit for what is happening because it feels as though a deeper intelligence is almost doing it for us.

A state of deep concentration is not contingent on any circumstance or situation, the level of our skills or abilities or any particular way of thinking. Falling into 'the zone' is a natural part of being human. It is not caused by us doing anything. There is nothing to 'do'.

We fall effortlessly into 'the zone' and everything irrelevant disappears as we become fully immersed and energised in playing the game.

The concentration required for elite performance can be found in small children and teenagers as much as anywhere else:

- Small children will be happily engrossed in the simplest of activities, e.g. building a tower of bricks or putting together a puzzle
- Teenagers playing computer games become so lost in the virtual reality that they forget about their dinner and their homework

For children, concentration is not effortful, it is inevitable. They are not trying to concentrate; they do what instinctively feels right in the moment. When we fall into 'the zone' we did not decide to, it happens without realising.

We concentrate more on something when we are interested in it. The more we love what we are doing, the more we will effortlessly concentrate on it. When we love playing the game, there is nothing more interesting and nothing simpler than immersing ourselves in it. For example, for a batsman who loves batting, not because of the results or the status they might get but because they just love it, concentration is one of the most straight-forward things in the world. The illusions of how we will be affected by others' judgement or the consequences of our performances, do not seem to be a big issue when we are doing something that we love.

Most of the way adults approach concentration is in the completely opposite direction. We pick up misunderstandings and develop habits of thinking that make concentrating feel harder than it is. We forcibly make an effort to concentrate, we try to 'switch on' or use a mental technique to try to focus or quieten the mind. This only makes things harder as we add more of the only thing that is preventing an effortless absorption in the moment – thought. Then we use more thinking to criticise ourselves when we fail to match up to a made-up measurement of how focused we should have been.

When we are analysing and judging everything we do or what we think will happen, all this thinking gets in the way of experiencing a state of mind where we play freely with little on our minds. In our formative experiences of playing sport, we played in the backyard for the sheer enjoyment of competing in that moment. Playing the game 'in the zone' was completely natural and intuitive to us before our minds became full of expectations, goals and ideas of how we think things ought to be. Athletes who play the game as they did when they were children have little concern about the story that they and other people are making up about what it means. They enjoy the game for what it is.

THOUGHT FLOWS TO, AND FROM, CLARITY TO CLUTTERED ON ITS OWN

High performance is termed being in 'flow' for a reason. The mind is not meant to be in a fixed state. When the mind is allowed to flow from calm, focused and in 'the zone' to agitated, nervous and over-thinking we are capable of far more than we ever are when we are fighting or trying to control our experience.

If we try to control the natural fluctuations of thought, we will only think ourselves into clutter with more thinking. We cannot think ourselves into a good mood. However, we can prolong low moods with an overuse of thinking. Similarly, we cannot think ourselves into the present moment on the field of play, only out of it. If we try not to think, this effort only creates more thinking (e.g. the instruction, "Don't think about pink elephants" almost always leads to people thinking about pink elephants!).

Falling into the zone is natural. Trying to get there only makes it more elusive. We fall into 'the zone' when all our thinking quietens – not because we quieten it ourselves, but because the mind is designed to self-correct to clarity. When good moods and 'the zone' occur, it is a natural process of the mind self-correcting and thought disappearing so that all that is left are the innate states of well-being and concentration.

"You cannot, at the same time, concentrate and think about concentrating."

—Alan Watts (Philosopher).

We do not need to deliberately create a process or routine to concentrate. Human beings are creatures of habit and we have naturally occurring routines for all sorts of things, but they are not the cause of our state of mind. Obsessively deliberate processes and routines unnecessarily fill our minds with thinking about everything that needs to be in place before we can play. We do not need to follow a set routine of thoughts or behaviours for hitting a ball any more than we need one for cleaning our teeth. If a routine or process naturally occurs to us and feels right, then there is common-sense in following it. However, we already have the psychological capacity to concentrate, we just have to *know* it.

Concentration involves being more aware of one thing rather than another. It is natural and intuitive to move our attention from one place to another. Everyone's awareness drifts from time to time. Concentration drifts, not because of what we are thinking about, but when we are distracted by our thinking. There are no distractions except for thought itself. When we are lost in our thinking about the past or the future, we are not in the present moment. As we fall out of, or take less notice of, our thinking, by just getting on and playing the game, then we fall back into the moment.

Concentration will go up and will go down. The more we attempt to control it, the more thinking we create. As we let go of trying to control our attention, we can do what feels right in the moment, knowing that we do not need to do anything except watch the ball and hit it. As we keep playing, our concentration falls effortlessly into a deeper focus without us noticing.

Our best performances come to the surface when we get on with playing the game without trying to force or control how we are thinking or feeling. It is OK not to be in 'the zone', we are always capable of adapting and finding a way to perform from where we are. Understanding that nobody can, or needs to, stay there forever takes away feeling the need to strive for and work at it. It leaves us with the freedom to play without the illusory idea that we have to be thinking (or feeling) a certain way.

PLAYING INSTINCTIVELY

"It was not by design at all. It was just simply intuition. It was not based on science or analysis or thought or design. It was all by instinct. It happened one day at a competition. My mind was driving my body to work out the best way to get over the bar."

—Dick Fosbury (High Jump – pioneer of the 'Fosbury Flop' technique).

Our instincts know how to play the game better than 'we' (our intellect/conscious thinking) do. We can hit or kick a ball well without having to think about it. When we are playing at our absolute best, it is as if we are not actually doing it but it is happening *through* us.

Instinct is the intelligence that allows us to play without consciously thinking about what to do or how to do it, allowing us to play our best game despite having little idea about how we did it. This is why some of the best players say things like, "All I do is see ball, hit ball" because, whilst all top-level sport is obviously far more complex than that, when we are playing instinctively that is how simple it seems.

This innate, instinctive intelligence is not to be confused with the intellect – our capacity for analytical thinking – that evolves as we grow older allowing us to make comparisons and judgements and to memorise information. When we are playing on instinct, the game is enjoyable and our movements and performance flow. We have a deep sense of faith in what to do and how to do it.

Instinct is the difference between when we *know* something is right and when we *think* it might be. It is a constant intelligence that exists at a deeper level than the ever-changing thoughts that occur to us. It shows up as a gut feeling, common-sense and taking action without a logical reason how or why but because it just feels right. One thing naturally (and instinctively) follows another before we then look back and see what a great performance, idea or decision came from it, despite so little conscious awareness of the thinking that preceded it.

Our instincts allow skills to be performed naturally, no matter how we are feeling. When we play instinctively, allowing what comes naturally to flow, our potential rises beyond the limitations of how well we think we can play. It allows "I did not know I could do that!" experiences to take place. We have thoughts that tell us we cannot do something, but when we get into it, instinct takes over and we find that we are able to after all! To trust our instincts, we only have to understand that this amazing, innate intelligence is always available to us.

As we gain more insight into the nature of concentration, the more we find ourselves falling back into 'the zone' – and the less bothered we are if we do not. If we are sitting lost in our thoughts and out of the corner of our eye, we see a tennis ball coming towards us, then there is a good chance that we will instinctively turn and catch it. How much concentration did we need to catch the ball? None. Our instincts automatically engage us into the present moment. We can trust our instincts to come through for us whether we are immersed in the moment, or whether we are struggling to find our rhythm of playing. All we need is to realise that they are always there, no matter how complicated our thoughts and feeling are making it look in the moment.

Playing with freedom and expressing ourselves on the field are natural. It is playing the game as it intuitively resonates with, and makes sense to, us. In backyard games, players compete without inhibitions or second-guessing themselves. Instead, they experiment with new methods and strategies to be successful. Backyard games are no less competitive than any formal or structured competition, often they are more so. In these games, we play each moment unburdened from the past or the future because we are simply absorbed in it. This freedom is the space that allows our skills to flow naturally, with an instinctive sense of what to do, where to be and how to perform.

"I've learned to trust my subconscious. My instincts have never lied to me. I have no technique on my mind, I just let it go."

—Tiger Woods (Golf – winner of 14 'Majors').

'CHOKING' IS THE OPPOSITE OF THE 'THE ZONE'

'Choking' in sport occurs when the execution of a normally habitual set of movements deteriorates to the point where a skilled player becomes unable to perform to a fraction of their usual ability. It often occurs when the athlete most wants to play at their best level.

It is an unintentionally learned phenomenon that occurs when we experience a low state of mind during a game (e.g. a state of heightened anxiety) and we try to think our way out of this state. We attempt to fix how we are feeling or control the movements required for performance. However, instead of having the desired effect, the increased thinking only compounds the feeling of tension and our movements (and the results they create) become more unnatural and less effective. The harder we try, the worse it gets.

A low state of mind cannot lead to choking on its own. It happens when we believe the thinking that we have (e.g. 'I feel under pressure because I'm winning' or 'because this is a big match') and try to control our movements or fix the feeling with yet more thinking. All this thinking overcomplicates something that came so naturally to us before. Rather than trusting our instincts, our performance chokes as we try to take control of the movements with our intellect.

If we are feeling under pressure and do not understand where the feeling is coming from then it may appear logical to try to change the feeling. However, the attempt to fix or change how we are feeling only pours more fuel of thinking on to the fire of the feeling we are already experiencing. An occasion, an opponent or a crowd cannot cause certain states of mind nor choking. These circumstances are all inherently neutral, even if they are seemingly big crowds, aggressive opponents or career defining occasions. Only thought creates the meaning and feeling we attribute to them.

Our thinking can look compelling and, if we begin to get caught up in our panicked thinking about the game, we forget about the instinctive intelligence that is always capable of hitting, catching or bowling the ball. 'Choking' occurs when we do not know that we have this deeper instinctive intelligence, or when we doubt or mistrust it. We can get caught 'in two minds' on what decision to make because we are listening to the random, flustered thoughts that are occurring to us rather than trusting what comes naturally.

THE MORE WE THINK THAT SOMETHING OUTSIDE OF US CAN CREATE A FEELING WITHIN US, THE MORE WE WILL THINK ABOUT IT

If we believe a circumstance determines how we feel, we will try to move towards certain situations and change or avoid others. This *trying* only revs up more thinking, prolonging the illusion we are experiencing.

If we arrive at a Cup Final and think that this 'big occasion' can make us feel under pressure, then we will think more about it. If we hear the crowd chanting and believe that their noise can make us feel under pressure, then we will think more about it. If we think that being in the lead in a championship can put us under pressure, we will more think about it. If we believe that making a mistake can make us feel under pressure then we will think about mistakes, and if we make a mistake, we will do even more thinking about that mistake in the hope of avoiding another one. It is all of this thinking that is the actual cause of feeling under pressure.

Being able to analyse a game situation and opponents is a key skill for performance but relying on this intellectual thinking can get in the way of our ability to perform naturally and instinctively. If we become dependent on our intellect, we can become so used to trying to think our way through situations that we forget a more natural and easier learning process exists. We are likely to take our perceptions of the game quite seriously, taking failures personally and to heart as we habitually analyse our interpretations of events and ruminate on our mistakes.

Our intellect is a great tool to assess, compare and plan. Our continual calculations mean we can adjust to situations. However, relying on it above our instincts often leaves us limited to strict parameters where we believe that the risk is worth the potential reward. This can lead us to becoming somewhat robotic and inflexible at times – "I do it this way and it works" or "this is the way I am" – and therefore we can struggle to succeed on occasions which call for us to adapt.

For all the calculations our intellect can carry out, its attempts to control movement are counter-productive. When left to instinct, our skills do very nicely on their own. The more thinking we add, the further we move away from a natural and effective performance. Analysis is great, but there is a time and a place. We only have to consider how difficult and complicated walking down the stairs can become if we are thinking hard enough about every single movement required. Doing lots of thinking about something is OK. However, once we have learned from it, doing less is almost always easier and more productive.

WE DO NOT HAVE TO DO ANYTHING ABOUT NERVES

Some people hate feeling nervous before a game and feel it really inhibits them. Others love it, feeling that nerves give them a buzz which helps them to play their best. The truth is that nerves are neither good nor bad. Problems arise, not from being nervous, but when we believe that being nervous is bad for us or it means that we will not perform.

During the South Africa vs. West Indies One Day International in 2015:

AB de Villiers: "Someone else should bat."

"What?" asked his team-mate Faf du Plessis.

"The nerves, I always get so nervous before I bat," replied De Villiers.

Eventually a wicket falls and de Villiers had to go in. As he made his way down the stairs, he tripped and stumbled.

There were 69 balls left in the innings when De Villiers arrived at the crease.

He faced 44 of them and scored 149, making the fastest ODI century in just 31 balls.

> ***"[When I'm waiting to bat] I can't wait to get out there and am full of nervous energy. It's good though because nervous energy is great energy; it means you care about what you're doing and are zeroed in on what you've got to do."***
>
> ***—Kevin Pietersen (8181 Test runs for England at an average of 47).***

Nerves are not a predictor of a lack of success, although sometimes we can think that they are. Despite how compelling the thoughts of worst-case scenarios look, feeling nervous does not mean what we are thinking about will happen. A feeling of nervousness, anxiety or panic is always, and only, informing us the degree to which our minds are full of busy over-thinking.

Becoming comfortable being uncomfortable is a by-product of knowing that feeling uncomfortable (e.g. nervous, anxious, afraid) is OK. It is a natural product of the fluctuations in thought that pass without us needing to do anything. The more we see that we are capable of having a thought or feeling (i.e. a tempo-rary illusion in our experience) without having to respond to it, we return to playing naturally one moment at a time.

There is no way to avoid the feeling of nervousness because thought builds up for everyone at times. We cannot control the thoughts that pop into our head nor can we just clear our minds – if anyone could, we would all be doing it. We will feel nervous until we do not – which is usually the point of the game where we do not have time to entertain our nervous thinking. However, we can always see what is occurring for what it is – thought in the moment – so that we automatically drop misunderstandings and feeling nervous loses its power over us.

The game does not change just because we are feeling anxious. We can have a lot of nervous thinking about the occasion, the opponent or the crowd and understand that is just a collection of thoughts. We do not have to believe any given thought; we do not have to act on it. We can laugh at it, ignore it or live it with and play on anyway. We can have a million different thoughts going on inside our heads and still smash the ball out of the park, because no thought can affect how capable we are except when we believe an insecure thought to be true and act on it.

THERE IS A SIMPLE EXPLANATION OF WHY PEOPLE CRUMBLE UNDER THE FEELING OF PRESSURE – THEY MISUNDERSTAND IT

Feeling under pressure *looks* like it leads to mistakes or choking, but it cannot. Pressure is a normal feeling coming from the thinking we have in the moment. Some people feed off the feeling of pressure to perform, others find it extremely inhibiting. It is the same feeling but everyone's relationship to it is different. Experiencing excessive amounts of pressure that seems debilitating means that we have an excessive amount of misunderstood thoughts and beliefs about performance getting in our way. We neither need the feeling of pressure, nor do we need to avoid it. It is inevitable that we will experience it. Yet there is nothing we need to do about it.

Sport *looks* like it creates pressure, but it cannot. There is no pressure in kicking, hitting or bowling a ball, or in running, jumping and catching. The feeling of pressure will always arise in a low state of mind and disappear in a higher mood, regardless of how good we are, how challenging our circumstances or how important we believe them to be.

When our state of mind is lower it is likely that the situation will look tougher and more important, and the sense of expectation and needing to perform will feel heavier. When our state of mind is higher, the same game will look like a challenge or great fun. If a game feels pressurised it is because in that moment, we *think* the game is creating pressure not because it actually is. As soon as a game feels like pressure it is a sure-fire sign that our thinking has got ahead of us.

'The zone' is a state of mind where we lose ourselves in the moment. We perform effortlessly when we are completely immersed in the game so that our sense of self, ideas, concepts and beliefs fall away. We are left intuitively responding to what occurs moment to moment as our performance flows on instinct. 'Choking' is the complete opposite phenomenon where an obsession with ourselves leads to losing our bearings. We pay attention to our thoughts about "What will other people say?", "Am I good enough?" or "Will I get dropped if I fail?" to such a degree that we become disconnected from the game and lose sight of what truly powers performance.

When we 'choke', the performance has become all about us, as we get wrapped up in our thoughts, feelings, anxieties and attempts to control it. When we play in the zone, our best performances seem to have very little to do with us at all. There is greater instinctive power doing the 'heavy lifting' for us.

Feeling pressure is not a problem. The issue is getting so lost in the feeling that we buy into the illusory, powerless thinking taking place, and forget that our instincts allow us to perform no matter how we are feeling. The more we see pressure for what it is, our potential to perform, with or without the feeling, rises. Sometimes it feels simple and at other times, it feels complicated. Either way, we are still capable of executing our skills.

Trying to control anything – our movements, our thoughts, our lives – only has the opposite effect. There is no state of mind that is a guarantee of success, so there is nothing to seek. There is no state of mind that is a disaster, so there is nothing to run from. When we understand all of that, it is amazing what can happen when we let go of trying to control everything and get into the game trusting that we can just play.

"When I, or any batsman, is in his nineties, we can start over-thinking, 'How do I get there, what shot do I play? And that is not good. You just need to let it flow. Virender Sehwag did that so well. He got to 100s, 200s and 300s with a six or a four. He just executed. When you let it go, it becomes a cakewalk."

—Kumar Sangakkara (Cricket – scored more than 30,000 international runs).

WINNING THE CRITICAL MOMENTS

Great players seize the moments that define games. From scoring a match-winning free-kick in football, to absorbing an intense spell of bowling in cricket or shifting the momentum of a point in tennis, the best players rise to the moment and bring their best play to the game when they need it most.

BEING ABLE TO PERFORM CONSISTENTLY IN THE KEY MOMENTS OF GAMES COMES FROM SEEING THAT THESE MOMENTS HOLD NO POWER OVER US

Even when there is a lot on the line and everything comes down to one moment, it is impossible for that moment or its consequences to create a feeling of pressure within us. Whilst we may have placed a great deal of importance on a moment, it is inherently neutral; it simply is what it is. In that moment, players who understand the inside-out nature of their experience will either feel pressure but know that a feeling alone has no power to throw them off their game or they will be so absorbed in the game that they do not even think about it, they just do it.

A penalty kick, a World Cup or Olympic Final or needing 4 runs to win off the last ball are all incredibly challenging, but they have no control over us and how we feel, unless we believe they do. The bigger deal that we believe a moment to be, the more thinking we will carry about that game or that moment. This is fine as long as we see it for what it is.

We can deeply want to perform and to win whilst understanding that every moment in the game is powerless to determine our experience. For example, missing a penalty kick or getting hit for 6 cannot, on its own, make us feel anything. It is understandable why people react how they do to such game events, but it is always, and only, our thinking about the event that is giving us an experience of it.

If we are busy thinking about the mistake we made five minutes ago, we are mentally in a place other than the game. We do not have to attach to one interpretation of the game and make it a habit (e.g. believing that mistakes make us less of a person so every time we make a mistake, we react to our thinking about it by dropping our head and becoming uninterested in the game). If we throw our bat or racquet in frustration during a game, it is because we are reacting to our thinking about something that is now in the past. We will keep feeling as frustrated for as long as we keep energising the thinking we have about what has happened.

A similar phenomenon can occur even when we are doing well. If we hit a great shot and spend so long basking in the glory of it, the game can pass us by until our attention is back on what is happening now. Whether it was one minute or one year ago, the past is not relevant to us being able to perform in, and enjoy, this moment right now. Every moment of the game is a new opportunity to play it afresh, as it comes.

Making mistakes and being outplayed at times are inevitable. We are human, not perfect. Whatever happens on the field, when it's gone, it's gone; unless we keep bringing it back into our experience. The event itself has no power over us; it is only how we think about it and how much we pay attention to that thinking.

The best way to move on is to simply keep playing and, as we do, what happens next will take care of itself. Not every game can be perfect, but we are always able to perform more than we think we can. Every moment, ball or play in the game creates a new chance to be the best we can be. As we fall deeper into the moment, our abilities and skills come to the fore and we begin to do things that we did not know that we were even capable of.

THE VARIABLES OF EACH GAME (OPPONENTS, OFFICIALS, CONDITIONS) ARE BEYOND OUR CONTROL, BUT WE CAN ALWAYS ADAPT AND FIND A WAY TO PERFORM

Most of the 'mind games' in sport are based on trying to get people to believe that there is psychological pressure where none exists. Some players relish a verbal battle of sledging and trash-talk. Some players hate it. Trash-talk is an attempt to get someone else drawn into thinking about the game, rather just playing it. It is not the words or the tone that they are spoken in that cause discomfort, but our own interpretation of it in the moment and the stories that we create about it (e.g. "They can't say that about me!").

We can respond to sledging in any number of ways, none any more 'right' than the other. What is important is that we understand that somebody else's words cannot cause us to feel a certain way. We might feel intimidated if someone is in our face and bawling at us, but what is happening does not directly lead to how feel about it. Depending on the thinking they have, some people will hate that experience, but some might relish it.

When we forget that it is our own thinking about the situation causing the feelings we have in the moment, we can easily become consumed in that thinking about how someone is behaving or what they are saying (or any other external circumstance or situation). This only serves to make us feel worse and we can lose attention on performing our skills. However, if, in that moment, we intuitively understand that it is impossible for another person to directly make us feel intimidated, then whatever is happening loses its power psychologically.

Our ability to adapt to the conditions, rather than feeling a victim of them, can turn any game in our favour. Adaptability is in our nature. Our ability to adapt on the field, in the moment, is dependent on our capacity to see something new – to have a fresh thought about how to play.

There are conditions that suit some players and teams better than others. We do not need to kid ourselves or ignore the reality of the situation; we just have to play better regardless. The conditions are an issue only to the extent that we think about them and see those thoughts as real. The conditions will never be perfect and, even when they are, there is no guarantee that they will lead to success. We can only ever play the hand that we have been dealt. We might wish the game was more in our favour, but we still remain capable of playing to the best of our ability.

Getting wrapped up in the difficulty of the game is never going to be more productive than playing each ball, moment or point with an open mind. In any game, even if one player or team has a 99% chance of winning, there is still a 1% chance that they will not. This means that all the thinking we have to the contrary – "they're better", "I'm going to lose" – is as made-up as every other thought we have. We do not need to change the thinking we have. We only need to see it for what it is, play the game and drag that 1% chance upwards one point at a time.

"It doesn't matter how many games you've played or what you've done before, you still go out on nought every time you bat whether you're playing your first game or your 150th. It doesn't get any easier. But that's why it's called Test cricket. It's meant to be hard."

—Alastair Cook (Cricket – England's all-time record Test Match run scorer).

THE MORE PLAYERS UNDERSTAND THE GAME AND THEIR INDIVIDUAL ABILITIES, THE MORE HELPFUL SOLUTIONS OCCUR TO THEM IN MATCHES

Decision making is a by-product of our understanding of our game and the game situation we are in. A player's tactical awareness of the game – understanding their own strengths and weaknesses and how to adapt to different opponents in varied conditions – will determine the decisions they make in matches. The more we understand our abilities and the nuances of the game itself, the more the solutions that occur to us when we are on the field will be useful, insightful and allow us to effortlessly make a productive decision.

At the top level the margins for error are so small that intuitively understanding the risk and reward of the options available to us, given our abilities, makes a key difference in performance. When our tactical understanding is low, the potential solutions that occur to us to deal with the challenges within the game, will be less effective. Therefore, players may seem to make panicked decisions because a low risk, high reward, common-sense solution has not occurred to them.

Almost every athlete can explain what they would have done differently after the game, but not all learn and do it better the next time that they are in a similar situation. This is because most do not look to how their understanding of the nature of thought in creating their moment-by-moment experience, as well as their game understanding, is the root cause of the decisions they make. It is always easier to look for an excuse or to go back to working on our skills, but sometimes the biggest learning curve comes from looking a bit deeper.

Everybody has the capacity to understand the game more clearly, but not everyone seeks out that possibility. Therefore, some players continually learn from their experiences and begin to seem very 'smart' athletes, while other players make the same mistakes season after season. Complex games require an element of 'figuring it out' that can be turned into our game plans. If we do not appreciate and engage in that process, then adapting to differing game situations becomes difficult and our choices can seem reckless.

Analysis can be a huge help in preparing for games. Our intellect allows us work out the strengths and weaknesses of the opposition, to develop effective game plans and plays a crucial role in the learning process in complex environments. However, decision making on the field of play comes down to trusting what we *know* to be the right option, even if we cannot explain why. Without instinct, we would not be capable of anything on the sports field.

The value is in knowing the value that both our innate, instinctive intelligence and our intellectual, analytical intelligence bring to our sporting performances. Our capacity to 'play smart' rises as we let go of our misunderstandings about pressure and performance that cause unhelpful patterns of thinking. Then we can assess, and play, match situations based on reality and not on illusory worries about the game or its consequences.

> *"5 percent of the time your opponent is in the zone and you won't win; 5 percent of the time you're in the zone and can't lose. But the other 90 percent of the time it's up for grabs; there is a way to win. You've just got to figure out what it is."*
>
> *—Andre Agassi (Tennis – 8 Grand Slam titles).*

TOP PERFORMERS UNDERSTAND THE VALUE OF 'BEING THEMSELVES'

The best players put in the hours and effort again and again to cultivate their craft. Analysis, purposeful practice, competitive matches, coaches' advice and learning from other players all play their part. However, our game is our own. There is nothing more valuable than our own understanding and our own intuition. This provides us with the openness and curiosity to develop an instinctive way of playing the game based on our body, our rhythm and our enjoyment.

There are a million different ways to achieve the same outcome. Whilst there are some commonalities between the best performers, every great has a method that is intuitively natural to them. Roger Federer does not play tennis like Rafael Nadal and Cristiano Ronaldo does not play football like Lionel Messi. The more comfortable we become in ourselves, and in our own style of playing the game, the more effective decisions we will make because we will not spend time second guessing ourselves.

When we are trying to protect our ideas about ourselves and what we perceive others' opinions of us to be, we can be more concerned with trying play in a way that we think is more stylish or how others want us to play. However, finding a way to being as effective as possible always tells over time in sport, regardless of how it looks. In the long run, it does not matter who plays the game in the most conventional or aesthetically pleasing manner. What matters is being able to perform time after time, day after day, however it looks or whatever anyone else thinks. Each player's individual style then emerges naturally from their pursuit of substance on the field of play.

There is no process, technique or strategy that is guaranteed to work for any individual, no matter how well it worked for somebody else. Trying to follow a prescribed method – including *trying* to be more instinctive – will lead only to more thinking rather than more success. Effortless decisions come from being ourselves, understanding the game and having faith in our own answers.

Our strengths are what make us the player that we are. When we really understand our strengths, we intuitively play to them when matches are on the line. In periods where our results are not matching up to our expectations, it becomes easy to forget our strengths or to believe that the way somebody else plays the game is the only way to succeed.

Athletes find a method that works for them when they understand and apply the abilities they have at that moment, rather than worrying about what they cannot do. This occurs as we test and stretch our strengths so that we can clearly see both the options that they provide us with in the game and their limitations. This allows us to build our game plans around them, to exploit what we do best and to limit the opportunities for our opponents. When we understand our strengths, keeping it simple is a natural by-product. We can overcomplicate the game with doubts and judgement to the extent that we forget how simple sport can be when we play to our strengths.

Our understanding of our game grows when we appreciate how and when to use our skills to perform even when we are not at our fluent best. The game itself becomes simpler, and our strengths become clearer, when we remember that the game is made up of running, hitting, kicking, jumping, catching or throwing and not the story that we tell ourselves about whether we think we are good enough or not or what we think will happen if we succeed or fail.

"You learn that there's no right way to do it, no wrong way to do it. It's just what you feel comfortable with, to trust that."

—Steph Curry (Basketball – NBA Most Valuable Player 2015 & 2016).

WE ALWAYS HAVE NOTHING TO LOSE BUT THE GAME

It is great to win but our results are not the only definition of success worth playing sport for. It is possible to have a far broader appreciation of what we have gained from playing sport, including the people we meet, the places it enables us to visit and the things we learn about ourselves and the game. We may accomplish everything we set out to and have millions in the bank, but it will not determine our feelings of well-being. That, we have already.

Competition is an endless feedback loop of where we are at and what we can do to get better. The more our opponents tests us, the greater the opportunity there is to learn, improve and find the outer edges of our potential. Whether we see our opponent as an obstacle or an opportunity depends on the thinking we have about them. Becoming the best we can be is dependent on having opponents who can challenge our skills, tactics, fitness and ability perform when the game is on the line, to higher and higher levels.

The ability to solve problems and be creative only diminishes when we become so lost in our thinking that the situation looks hopeless. Then we have no psychological space left open for seeing the situation in a new way or having fun and seeing how the game plays out. When our perspective naturally expands, the game feels like a game again and not as though we have the weight of the world resting on our shoulders.

The best players fight for every point and never seem to know when they are beaten, because they do not give any time to contemplating whether the game is unwinnable. They are so committed to each moment that if they have a thought that suggests they should give up, it simply makes no sense. They play every point full out because being immersed in the game and pushing themselves to their limits is its own reward.

Performance is about leaving no stone unturned and having fun. One without the other is unfulfilling. We do not control the result. We can improve, prepare and give it everything we can to win, but we do not control how it is going to play out. We can only fully commit ourselves to competing and the pursuit of our potential. From there, the ebb and flow of the game will take its course.

In the grand scheme of a 13.8-billion-year-old universe, how we perform on the sports field only matters so much. We can think the game is so important that we forget the simple enjoyment of playing it and our good fortune to be here. Being able to see that the game is unlikely to matter as much as we think it does, bring us back to reality.

The deeper our understanding of thought, pressure and performance, the broader our perspective on the game will be. Perspective involves understanding that, whilst our thoughts, feelings and results will inevitably change, our capacity to be ourselves and to have fun and perform remains constant.

Playing our game is a vehicle to experience everything that is already a part of who we are – well-being, resilience, motivation, confidence and the capacity to perform to our potential. When the match is over, whether we have won, lost or drawn, we are still OK at the deepest level. When we know that, we are free to play and enjoy the game as if it is everything whilst knowing that it is not.

"We live on a blue planet that circles around a ball of fire, next to a moon that moves the sea, and you don't believe in miracles?"

—Anonymous.

IN SUMMARY

Our experience – feelings, emotions and perceptions – can appear to be created by what is happening in our lives or in the world. However, it only ever occurs from the inside-out, from the ever-changing nature of thought we have in each moment.

The misunderstanding that pressure comes from outside of us (from the game or the consequences) can create infinite patterns of unhelpful thinking. The more strongly we believe an outside-in illusion (e.g. our well-being is dependent on good performances or earning lots of money) to be true, the more pressure we will feel because we will do more thinking about them.

When we understand where our feelings and experience are coming from, misunderstanding falls away of its own accord because it no longer makes sense. The more clearly we understand the nature of thought and how the mind works, the more straight-forward it is to appreciate the ups and downs of our journey.

We will all feel pressure at times, because thought fluctuates for everyone. To understand pressure is to know that feeling under pressure cannot inhibit our performances except if we believe it can. We experience more concentration, motivation, resilience and confidence as we understand their innate nature.

Sometimes performing feels natural and easy and sometimes it feels tough, but either way we can always find a way to perform and be the best we can be in that moment. We can trust our instincts, use our intellect and enjoy ourselves. As our understanding – of our experience, ourselves and the game – deepens, its implications follow.

Just play. Just be you.

ACKNOWLEDGMENTS

My thanks and appreciation go to:

My wife Rachel for being you. For all your proof-reading, support and patience whilst I have been writing this book.

My father Brian for your editing and feedback for the book and for nurturing a love of sport in myself and my brother, Dan.

My mother Carole who inspired a love of books.

Mark Fenton for your initial feedback and for the opportunity to work for Bucks Cricket five years ago.

Sam Jarman for guidance on publishing and our ongoing discussions about the inside-out understanding.

Every player I have ever been fortunate to coach and every coach I have been fortunate enough to work with. I have learned so much from you all.

FURTHER RESOURCES

If the ideas in this book connected with you, I whole-heartedly recommend the resources below:

Books

The Enlightened Gardener by Sydney Banks

The Inside-Out Revolution by Michael Neil

The Path of No Resistance by Garret Kramer

The Three Principles of Outstanding Golf by Sam Jarman

The Untethered Soul by Michael A. Singer

Podcasts

The Primal Happiness Show

Waking Up the Neuroscience of Awareness

NB. The Inside-Out Understanding of the mind is also known as the Three Principles (of mind, consciousness and thought).

ABOUT THE AUTHOR

 Rich is Head Coach for the Buckinghamshire Cricket Board and a Performance Psychologist for Northamptonshire County Cricket Club.

He is an England & Wales Cricket Board Level 4 'Master Coach', with a Post-Graduate Diploma in Elite Cricket Coaching and has a Master of Science degree in Sport Psychology.

He lives in Northampton, England, with his wife Rachel. He is an avid follower of most sports, enjoys drinking a coffee or a pint of pilsner and days in the sun.

If you are interested in finding out more about the inside-out understanding of performance, feel free to contact Rich via twitter @rdhudson00, email at rdh00coaching@gmail.com or via his website www.rdh00.com.

Printed in Great Britain
by Amazon